Séverine Augé

Photographs by Fabrice Besse

Basics

VEGETABLES

———

Techniques, Tips, and 70+ Recipes to Confidently
Cook With Vegetables

Hardie Grant

NORTH AMERICA

Contents

Composing a Vegetarian Diet

The main challenge when adopting a vegetarian diet is maintaining an equivalent nutritional intake when replacing meat and fish with plant-based alternatives. So, what should you consider, and how can you compose meals with ease?

VEGETABLES AND FRUITS, YES— BUT THAT'S NOT ALL!

Having a varied diet is essential for preventing health deficiencies. To complement fruits and vegetables in a vegetarian diet, consider starchy foods (for energy throughout the day) and a variety of plant-based protein sources, such as legumes, oilseeds, and soybean derivatives. Varying the foods you consume is important for balanced nutrition. In addition to alternative sources of proteins, alternative sources of certain minerals (such as iron, zinc, and iodine) and vitamins (B12, in particular) must be considered.

50% fruits and vegetables

5% divided between fats and sugar

25% legumes, oilseeds, eggs, and dairy (protein sources)

Vitamin B₁₂

This vitamin is essential for proper functioning of the brain, nervous system, and immune system. It is considered the most challenging nutrient to source in a vegetarian diet because it can only be found in foods of animal origin. If you do not eat eggs or dairy products, consider taking a dietary supplement for this vitamin.

FOODS RICH IN VEGETABLE PROTEINS

<u>Legumes:</u> 5 to 10 grams of protein per 100 grams cooked
<u>Oilseeds:</u> 10 to 20 grams of protein per 100 grams raw
<u>Cereals:</u> 3 to 20 grams of protein per 100 g grams cooked
<u>**Fruits, vegetables, and mushrooms:**</u> 0.5 to 3 grams of protein per 100 grams raw

A well-balanced and quality vegetarian diet meets all the body's nutritional and energy needs.

20% starchy foods, such as cereals and tubers

9

A Vegetarian Pantry

For a varied diet, have ingredients at hand that are easy to integrate into your daily life and simple to prepare.

Cereals:
to keep you energized throughout the day
Rice (basmati, jasmine, whole grain or semi-whole grain), pasta (whole grain or semi-whole grain), bulgur, couscous, quinoa (three colors are available), bread (preferably whole grain or sourdough), buckwheat, oats...

Oilseeds, nuts, dried fruits:
for snacks, but that's not all
Seeds (sunflower, flax, sesame, pumpkin...) and nuts (almonds, hazelnuts, walnuts...) in the form of butters (almond butter, peanut butter...) or plant-based beverages. Dried fruits (apricots, figs, grapes...)

Other items to keep on hand
Cubes of organic vegetable stock; tomatoes as a paste, purée, and crushed; soy sauce; dried mushrooms; coconut milk; vinegars and oils; spices; condiments and pickles (mustard, gherkins, capers...); and canned vegetables, for a variety of choice throughout the year...

Supplies for every day:
to add more flavor to your dishes
Onions, garlic, shallots, fresh ginger, potatoes
(stored in the pantry), flour, starch, sugar,
chocolate, yeast, baking powder, baking soda,
salt, pepper, and aromatic herbs

Plant-based creams, milks, and cheeses
Plant-based beverages (oat, soy, almond...),
almond cream, and coconut cream

Legumes:
for quality proteins
Lentils, beans, chickpeas, split peas, fava beans—
dried or cooked (canned)

Soy products
Tofu, tempeh, plant-
based soy beverages

Alternatives to Animal Proteins

A person's recommended daily protein intake varies depending on age and gender. Choose legumes and oilseeds to complement proteins obtained from eggs, yogurt, and cheeses.

LEGUMES

These are plants that produce seed-bearing pods. The seeds can be dried for consumption and include lentils (red, green, black, yellow...), beans (pinto, kidney, navy beans...), fava beans, soybeans, and peas (split peas, chickpeas...).

To prepare them:

- Flavor the cooking water with an herb bouquet, single herbs, or large chunks of carrot or onion.
- Soak dried legumes for 12 to 24 hours before cooking them (except for lentils, which require only a brief rinse).

Fast Soak

Place the legumes in a saucepan and add three times their volume of water and 1 tablespoon baking soda. Bring to a boil. Once boiling, remove from the heat and let soak for 2 hours.

Lentils (red, green, black, yellow)

Plan about ⅓ cup / 75 g lentils per person. Rinse the lentils and place them in a saucepan with at least three times their volume of cold, unsalted water. Add some herbs, if desired. Bring to a boil and continue boiling throughout the cooking time.

Cooking

- *Green and black lentils: 20 to 25 minutes*
- *Yellow lentils: 35 minutes*
- *Red lentils: 10 to 15 minutes*

Season the lentils while they are still warm.

Beans and peas

Soaking time 12 to 24 hours
⅓ cup / 70 g dried legumes per person
Baking soda

Plan about ⅓ cup / 70 g dried beans or peas per person. Rinse the legumes and soak for 12 to 24 hours in a very large volume of cold water with 1 tablespoon baking soda. Drain, transfer to a saucepan, and add three times their volume of cold water and 1 teaspoon baking soda. Bring to a boil and continue boiling throughout the cooking time.

Cooking
- *White beans: 1 hour to 1 hour 20 minutes*
- *Red beans: 2 hours*
- *Kidney beans: 45 minutes to 1 hour 15 minutes*
- *Fava beans: 1 to 2 hours*
- *Chickpeas: 1 hour to 1 hour 30 minutes*
- *Split peas: 45 minutes to 1 hour*

To reduce the cooking time, use a pressure cooker and cut the recommended cooking time in half.

OILSEEDS

These come from plants that produce nuts and seeds that offer many benefits. They are rich in unsaturated fatty acids, and oils can be extracted from them (olive oil, hazelnut oil, sunflower oil...). These include seeds, such as flax, pumpkin, sunflower, and sesame, and nuts, such as pine nuts, pistachios, walnuts, hazelnuts, almonds, pecans, Brazil nuts, macadamia nuts, coconuts, and peanuts. All of these are rich in protein, fiber, minerals, and vitamins.

What are some ways to enjoy them?
In savory recipes:
- *whole, sprinkled atop stews (such as curry), soups, or salads*
- *as oils, offering variations in sauces and dressings*

In sweet recipes:
- *whole or puréed in hot breakfast cereals, on toast, or in granola*
- *as a plant-based beverage consumed as a drink or used for cooking*
- *as oils used in cake batters*

Eggs

Eggs are a true ally for vegetarians because they are a great source of protein. In addition to having significant nutritional value, they can be prepared in a variety of ways: hard-boiled, soft-boiled, poached, fried, scrambled, as an omelet, coddled...

Choosing the right eggs:

• <u>Freshness</u>: Fresh eggs can be eaten up to 28 days after laying. "Extra fresh" eggs are best for raw or partially cooked preparations (mayonnaise, tiramisu, soft-boiled...).

• <u>Size</u>: their size (from S for the smallest to XL or jumbo for the largest) is indicated on the carton. For baking, the weight of an egg out of the shell is considered to be 50 grams, which corresponds to a medium size (53 to 63 grams).

To cook eggs in their shells, bring a pan of water to a boil and carefully drop in the eggs. As soon as the water reaches a boil again, count
– 3 minutes for soft-boiled eggs (runny yolk)
– 6 minutes for soft-boiled eggs (soft yolk)
– 9 minutes for hard-boiled eggs

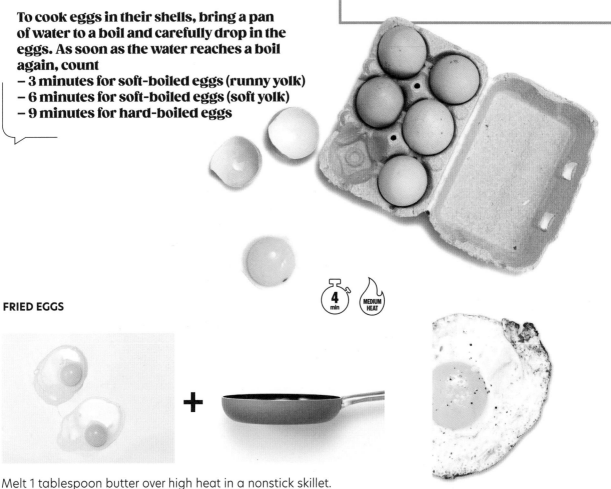

4 min · **MEDIUM HEAT**

FRIED EGGS

+

Melt 1 tablespoon butter over high heat in a nonstick skillet.
Crack 1 egg directly into the pan without breaking the yolk.
Reduce the heat to medium, and cook for 3 to 4 minutes. The egg is cooked when all of the white turns opaque.

SCRAMBLED EGGS

Crack 3 eggs into a bowl and briefly beat them. Pour into a saucepan and cook for 5 minutes over medium heat, stirring constantly. For creamy eggs, stop cooking 1 minute before they are done and stir in 1 tablespoon butter and 1 tablespoon crème fraîche.

MARINATED IN SOY

Bring a saucepan of water to a boil. Carefully place 4 eggs in the boiling water. When the water reaches a boil again, set a timer for 5 minutes. Transfer the eggs to a bowl of cold water to stop the cooking, then gently peel them. Combine 1 cup / 240 ml water, ⅔ cup / 150 ml soy sauce, and 2 tablespoons sugar. Place the eggs in the liquid and refrigerate for 24 to 48 hours to marinate.

OMELET

Crack 5 eggs into a bowl and briefly beat them. Add ⅔ cup / 150 ml cream, and season with salt and pepper. Melt 2 tablespoons butter in a nonstick skillet and pour in the eggs. Cook for 3 minutes over medium heat, fold in half, and cook for another 3 minutes for a runny omelet. For a well-cooked omelet, cover the pan with a lid and cook for another 2 minutes.

Flaky Pastry

For 1 tart **20 min** **20 min**

2 cups / 250 g
all-purpose flour

1 teaspoon fine salt

2½ teaspoons sugar

8½ tablespoons / 125 g
unsalted butter, slightly
softened and cubed

1 egg

 In a bowl, thoroughly combine
the flour, salt, and sugar.
Add the butter.

2 Work the dough for 3 minutes, rubbing it between
your hands to obtain a sandy texture: The butter
should be completely incorporated into the flour.

3 Add the egg and ⅓ cup / 80 ml cold water.
Knead to form a smooth dough.

4 Shape into a ball and cover. Set aside in the
refrigerator for least 20 minutes before use.

**An essential recipe for both savory and
sweet dishes.**

Pizza Dough

For 1 rectangular or 2 round

20 min

2 hrs 30 min

¾ teaspoon active dry yeast
1 tablespoon olive oil
2¼ cups plus 3 tablespoons / 300 g all-purpose flour
1 teaspoon fine salt

1 In a bowl, add just over ¾ cup / 200 ml warm water. Add the yeast, oil, flour, and salt.

2 Work by hand to form a homogeneous dough. Cover, and let stand at room temperature for 30 minutes.

3 Knead the dough again for a few minutes on a floured work surface. Cover with a clean cloth, and let stand at room temperature for about 2 hours.

4 Carefully spread the dough out onto a baking sheet. Add toppings, and bake on the upper rack at 475°F / 250°C for 10 to 12 minutes.

Sauces

These essential sauces are intended for any cook who wishes to enhance a salad, steamed vegetables, or platter of raw vegetables.

VINAIGRETTE

1 teaspoon grainy or fine mustard

2 tablespoons apple cider vinegar

¼ cup plus 2 tablespoons / 90 ml olive oil

Salt, pepper

In a bowl, vigorously combine the mustard, vinegar, and oil. Season with salt and pepper. Change up the oils and vinegars according to your tastes, while maintaining the same ratios. You can also enhance the vinaigrette with a few sprigs of chopped fresh herbs (chives, parsley, chervil...).

PESTO

2¾ oz / 80 g Parmesan cheese, cut into medium chunks

1½ oz / 40 g fresh basil

1 clove garlic, peeled

¼ cup plus 2 tablespoons / 50 g pine nuts

¼ cup / 60 ml good-quality olive oil

½ teaspoon flaky sea salt

Pepper

In a food processor, combine the Parmesan, basil, garlic, pine nuts, oil, and salt. Season with pepper. Process to the desired consistency. You can replace the pine nuts with other oilseeds (almonds, hazelnuts, cashews...) and the basil with other fresh herbs (parsley, cilantro, mint, tarragon...), as desired.

MAYONNAISE

1 large / 20 g egg yolk

1 tablespoon fine mustard

Just over ¾ cup / 200 ml neutral-flavored vegetable oil (a mixture of oils or sunflower oil)

Salt, pepper

In a bowl, whisk the egg yolk with the mustard. Gradually drizzle in a just few drops of oil at first while whisking. Once the texture is smooth, continue incorporating the oil in an increasingly larger stream while whisking. Season with salt and pepper. Cover with plastic wrap and refrigerate. Homemade mayonnaise can be kept for 24 hours in the refrigerator. If you want to make a larger quantity, use an electric mixer to make it easier.

Other sauces:

• <u>Peanut</u>: ¼ cup / 60 g peanut butter + 1 tablespoon soy sauce + ⅜-inch / 1 cm piece fresh ginger, grated + 1 teaspoon brown sugar. Dilute in a little hot water to the desired texture

• <u>Gribiche</u>: 1 hard-boiled egg + ¼ cup plus 2 tablespoons / 85 g mayonnaise + 1 handful chopped fresh herbs + 4 chopped gherkins + 1 dash lemon juice

• <u>Yogurt</u>: ½ cup / 125 g Greek yogurt + 1 handful chopped fresh herbs + 1 dash lemon juice + 1 clove garlic, finely chopped

• <u>Asian vinaigrette</u>: 2 tablespoons lime juice + ¼ cup plus 2 tablespoons / 90 ml sesame oil + 1 tablespoon honey + 1 teaspoon soy sauce

Loaded Bruschetta

👤 **4** 🥄 🕐 **4 min**

5 min

EQUIPMENT 1 cutting board and 1 knife
1 baking sheet

INGREDIENTS

14 oz / 400 g ripe tomatoes, assorted colors

1 clove garlic

10 pitted black olives

1 small loaf rustic bread

¼ cup plus 2 tablespoons / 90 ml olive oil

7 oz / 200 g burrata

4 sprigs basil

Salt, pepper

1 Dice the tomatoes, slice the olives into rounds, and halve the garlic. Slice the bread into thick slices.

2 In a large bowl, combine the tomatoes, olives, and ¼ cup plus 1 tablespoon / 75 ml of the oil. Season with salt and pepper.

3 Rub the bread slices with the garlic, season with salt and pepper, and drizzle with the remaining 1 tablespoon oil. Place the bread slices on a baking sheet and toast under the broiler for 3 to 4 minutes.

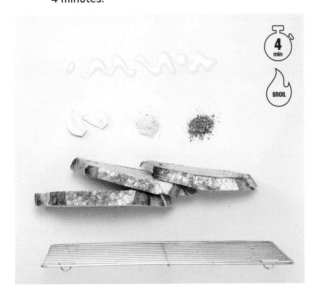

4 Arrange the tomatoes on top of the bread slices. Add pieces of burrata and a few basil leaves. Serve immediately.

Ideally, in step 2, let the tomatoes marinate for 1 hour for maximum flavor.

21

Dips

FOCUS

			EQUIPMENT	1 cutting board and 1 knife	1 food processor or blender
2-4	10 min	30 min		1 vegetable peeler	Aluminum foil
				1 baking sheet	Parchment paper

Baba Ganoush

2 eggplants • 4 cloves garlic • 3 tablespoons / 45 ml olive oil • 1 teaspoon cumin
1 tablespoon tahini (or 4 teaspoons golden sesame seeds crushed with 2 tablespoons
sunflower oil) • Salt, pepper

Cut the eggplants in half lengthwise and make a shallow crosshatch
pattern in the flesh using a small knife. Halve the garlic. Arrange each
eggplant half on a large sheet of aluminum foil, brush with the oil, and
sprinkle the cumin on top. Arrange the garlic around the halves. Season with
salt and pepper. Close up the foil and bake at 400°F / 200°C for 35 minutes,
or until soft when pierced with a knife. Scrape out the flesh using a spoon
and mash it with a fork, or process it in a food processor, with the roasted
garlic halves and the tahini.

Beet Hummus

12 oz / 350 g cooked beets • ¾ cup / 125 g canned chickpeas • 2 tablespoons
sunflower oil • 1 teaspoon ground coriander • 1¾ oz / 50 g fresh goat cheese
Salt, pepper

Cut the beets into large pieces. Drain the chickpeas. In a
food processor, process the beets, chickpeas, oil, coriander,
and cheese together until finely puréed. Season with salt
and pepper.

And for dippers? Raw vegetables cut into sticks, or tortillas lightly oiled and sprinkled with mild spices, and toasted in the oven at 375°F / 190°C for 10 minutes.

Guacamole

2 ripe avocados • 1 tomato • 1 red onion or shallot
8 sprigs cilantro • Juice of ½ lime • ½ teaspoon ground cumin
Salt, pepper

Dice the avocado flesh and the tomato. Chop the onion. Chop the cilantro. Using a fork, or a food processor, mash the avocado with the lime juice and cumin until creamy. Season with salt and pepper. Stir in the tomato and onion. To prevent oxidation, press the avocado pit into the guacamole and refrigerate in an opaque airtight container until ready to serve.

Roasted Carrot Hummus

14 oz / 400 g carrots • ⅔ cup / 100 g canned chickpeas
1 tablespoon fennel seeds • ¼ cup / 60 ml olive oil • Just over
¾ cup / 200 ml hot water • 1 tablespoon salted smoked almonds
Salt (optional), pepper

Peel the carrots and cut them into thick rounds. Drain the chickpeas. Combine the carrots, chickpeas, fennel seeds, and oil. Season with a little salt, if desired, and pepper. Place on a parchment paper-lined baking sheet and bake at 375°F / 190°C for 35 minutes. Transfer to a food processor and add the hot water. Process until very smooth. Served topped with the almonds.

Rösti-Style Frittata

4   **10 min**   **40 min**

EQUIPMENT
1 cutting board and 1 knife
1 grater
1 skillet

INGREDIENTS

2 onions

2 red bell peppers

6 sprigs parsley

14 oz / 400 g potatoes

3 tablespoons / 45 ml olive oil, plus a little more for cooking

6 large / 300 g eggs

Salt, pepper

1 Peel and thinly slice the onions. Remove the stem, seeds, and membrane from the peppers and cut the flesh into strips. Chop the parsley. Peel and grate the potatoes.

2 In a skillet, heat the 3 tablespoons / 45 ml oil over medium heat and cook the onions and peppers for 15 minutes, or until softened.

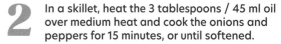

15 min

MEDIUM HEAT

3 In a bowl, combine the potatoes, cooked onions and peppers, parsley, and eggs. Season with salt and pepper.

4 Pour into a pan heated with a little more oil. Cook over low heat for 10 minutes on each side.

20 min

LOW HEAT

To have both sides crisp, start cooking in the pan over high heat, then bake at 350°F / 180°C for 15 minutes.

25

Samosas with Peas

4   **20 min**   **40 min**

EQUIPMENT

1 cutting board and 1 knife
1 skillet
1 baking sheet
1 basting brush
1 vegetable peeler

INGREDIENTS

4½ oz / 125 g potatoes
1 onion
2 cloves garlic
1¼-inch / 3 cm piece fresh ginger
2 sprigs mint
3 tablespoons / 45 ml oil, plus more for brushing
8 sheets brick dough (or phyllo dough)
1 teaspoon ground cumin
1 cup / 150 g frozen peas
1¾ oz / 50 g feta cheese
Salt, pepper

1

Peel the potatoes, onion, garlic, and ginger. Cut the potatoes into small cubes and chop the onion, garlic, ginger, and mint.

3 min

MEDIUM HEAT

2

In a skillet over medium heat, heat 2 tablespoons of the oil and sauté the onion, garlic, ginger, and cumin.

3

Add the potatoes and peas. Cover with water, and cook for 15 minutes over medium heat.

4

Drain. In a bowl, coarsely mash the mixture with the mint and feta. Season with salt and pepper.

5

Using a knife, cut the dough sheets in half. Fold the rounded ends toward the center to obtain a rectangular strip. Spoon 1 tablespoon of filling at one end and fold it over to close into a triangle. Lightly moisten the dough to help seal it. Repeat with the remaining strips.

6

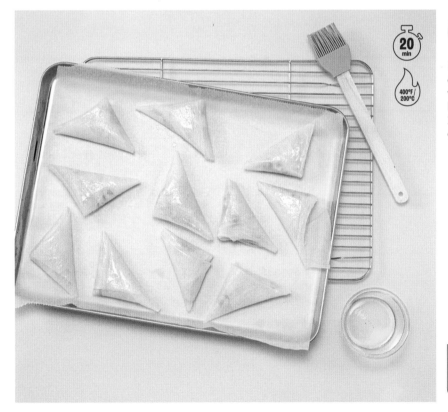

20 min

400°F / 200°C

Place the samosas on a baking sheet, brush with the remaining oil, and bake at 400°F / 200°C for 20 minutes, or until golden and crisp.

To adhere the ends closed, brush them with a little egg yolk.

Eggplant Rollatini

4   15 min   50 min

EQUIPMENT
1 cutting board and 1 knife
1 baking sheet
1 basting brush
1 strainer
1 casserole dish

INGREDIENTS

3 eggplants

1 clove garlic

9 oz / 250 g frozen chopped spinach, thawed

½ cup / 120 g ricotta

1 pinch nutmeg

¾ cup / 90 g grated Parmesan cheese

1 large / 50 g egg

⅔ cup / 150 ml tomato sauce

Olive oil

Salt, pepper

1 Cut the eggplants lengthwise into about ¼-inch / 5 mm strips. Peel and chop the garlic.

2 Place the strips on a baking sheet, brush with oil, and season with salt and pepper. Bake at 400°F / 200°C for 20 minutes.

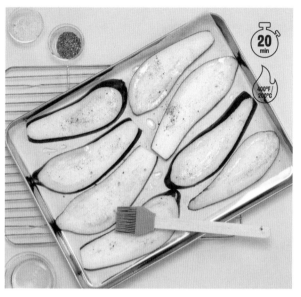

3 Press the spinach in a strainer to remove as much water as possible. Combine the spinach with the ricotta, garlic, nutmeg, ½ cup / 50 g of the Parmesan, and egg. Season with salt and pepper.

4 Spoon the filling onto the eggplant slices, roll them up, and arrange them snuggly in a casserole dish. Top with the tomato sauce and remaining Parmesan. Bake at 400°F / 200°C for 30 minutes.

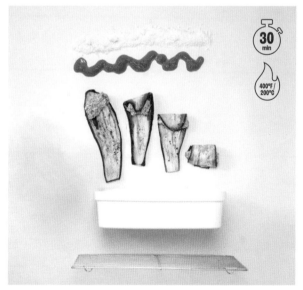

You can replace the ricotta with another fresh cheese of your choice, such as cottage cheese or a farmer's cheese.

Spring Rolls

4 **20 min** **5 min**

EQUIPMENT
1 cutting board and 1 knife
1 saucepan
1 skillet
1 kitchen towel

INGREDIENTS

2 leaves romaine lettuce
2 carrots
½ cucumber
6 sprigs cilantro
7 oz / 200 g firm tofu
4½ oz / 125 g rice
vermicelli noodles
2 tablespoons sunflower oil
2 tablespoons soy sauce
12 rice paper wrappers
Peanut Sauce (page 19)

1 Cut out the center rib from the lettuce leaves. Cut the carrots and cucumber into thin sticks. Remove the cilantro leaves from their stems. Cut the tofu into ⅜-inch / 1 cm thick sticks.

2 Place the vermicelli in a saucepan of hot water and soak for the time indicated on the package. Cool under cold running water, and set aside in a bowl of cold water.

3 In a skillet over high heat, heat the oil and fry the tofu for 5 minutes on all sides. Add the soy sauce and stir to coat the tofu well. Set aside.

4 Dip 1 rice paper wrapper in cold water. In the center, arrange a little of the lettuce, noodles, cucumber, carrots, tofu, and cilantro. Fold the wrapper sides in over the filling then roll forward tightly. Repeat and serve with the peanut sauce.

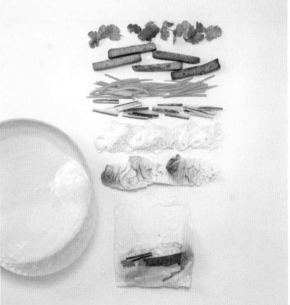

Veggie Cakes

INGREDIENTS

6 sprigs parsley
1 zucchini
3 carrots
1 potato
2 large / 100 g eggs
3 tablespoons / 25 g
all-purpose flour
2 tablespoons olive oil
Salt, pepper

4   15 min   25 min

EQUIPMENT
1 cutting board and 1 knife
1 strainer
1 vegetable peeler
1 baking sheet
Parchment paper

1 Chop the parsley. Very thinly slice (or grate) the zucchini. Peel and grate the carrots and potato.

2 Place the vegetables in a strainer and press firmly to remove as much water as possible.

3 In a bowl, combine the eggs, flour, vegetables, and parsley. Season with salt and pepper.

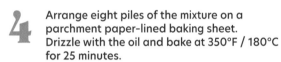

4 Arrange eight piles of the mixture on a parchment paper-lined baking sheet. Drizzle with the oil and bake at 350°F / 180°C for 25 minutes.

As an accompaniment, make a quick sauce by combining ⅔ cup / 150 g Greek yogurt, salt, pepper, the juice of ½ lemon, 1 clove chopped garlic, and a little chopped parsley.

Smashed Potatoes

👤 **4** 🥣 **10 min** 🕐 **1 hr**

EQUIPMENT
1 saucepan
1 baking sheet
Parchment paper

INGREDIENTS

2¼ lb / 1 kg waxy firm-flesh potatoes (such as Yukon Gold or yellow)

3½ tablespoons / 55 g unsalted butter, melted

9 oz / 250 g raclette cheese (or other melting Swiss cheese, such as Gruyère), sliced

1 Wash the potatoes. In a saucepan of salted water, boil the potatoes whole for 35 minutes. Check for doneness by piercing them with a knife.

2 Drain, then transfer the potatoes to a parchment paper-lined baking sheet. Press them to smash them. Brush with the melted butter and place them under the broiler until golden.

35 min

MEDIUM HEAT

BROIL

3 Add the cheese slices and place back under the broiler for 5 minutes.

5 min

BROIL

This recipe is a good option for raclette fans who do not own an electric raclette grill.

Vegetables & Mozzarella

👤 **4**

🥣 **5 min**

⏱ **25 min**

EQUIPMENT
1 cutting board and 1 knife
1 baking sheet
Parchment paper
1 strainer

INGREDIENTS

2 zucchini

2 eggplants

2 red bell peppers

2 red onions

¼ cup / 60 ml olive oil

1 teaspoon dried thyme

6 oz / 170 g artichoke hearts, in oil

10½ oz / 300 g mini mozzarella balls

3½ oz / 100 g arugula

Salt, pepper

1 Cut the zucchini and eggplants lengthwise into ¼-inch / 5 mm strips, the peppers into thin strips, and the onions into eight wedges.

2 Place the zucchini, eggplant, peppers, and onions on a baking sheet and brush them with the oil. Season with salt and pepper and sprinkle on the thyme. Bake at 375°F / 190°C for 25 minutes.

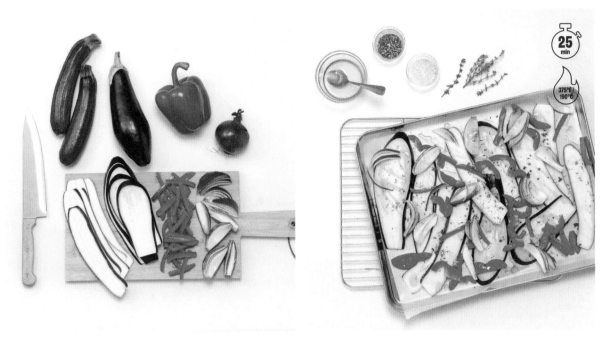

3

Remove from the oven. In a bowl, combine the roasted vegetables with the artichoke hearts, mozzarella balls, and arugula.

Halloumi Wraps

4

10 min

25 min

EQUIPMENT
1 cutting board and 1 knife
1 baking sheet
Parchment paper
1 skillet

INGREDIENTS
1 zucchini
1 small eggplant
1 red bell pepper
A few lettuce leaves
1 red onion
7 oz / 200 g halloumi cheese (or other cheese suitable for grilling)
3 tablespoons / 45 ml olive oil
4 flour tortillas
Juice of ½ lemon
9 oz / 250 g hummus
Salt, pepper

1 Cut the zucchini and eggplant into rounds, the pepper and lettuce into thin strips, the onion into thin wedges, and the halloumi into ¼-inch / 5 mm slices.

2 Place the zucchini, eggplant, pepper, and onions on a baking sheet, drizzle with some of the oil, and season with salt and pepper. Bake at 400°F / 200°C for 25 minutes. Warm the tortillas in the oven turned off.

3 Fry the halloumi in a little of the oil over high heat for 1 minute on each side. Add the lemon juice and stir to coat the cheese. Season with pepper.

4 Divide the hummus, lettuce, roasted vegetables, and fried cheese among the tortillas. Roll each tightly and cut in half diagonally.

Green Salad & New Potatoes

4

10 min

30 min

EQUIPMENT
1 baking sheet
1 saucepan
1 food processor

INGREDIENTS

1 lb 2 oz / 500 g new potatoes
¼ cup / 60 ml olive oil
3 sprigs thyme
1 cup / 150 g frozen peas
½ cup / 100 g frozen shelled fava beans
3½ oz / 100 g baby spinach

<u>For the herb dressing</u>

1¼ oz / 35 g fresh herbs (chives, chervil, dill...)
¼ cup / 50 g Mayonnaise (page 19)
Scant ½ cup / 100 g Greek yogurt
Juice of ½ lemon
Salt, pepper

1 Place the potatoes on a baking sheet. Drizzle with the oil and sprinkle on the thyme. Season with salt and pepper and bake at 400°F / 200°C for 30 minutes.

2 Cook the peas and beans for 5 minutes in a saucepan of boiling, salted water. Drain and immerse in a bowl of cold water.

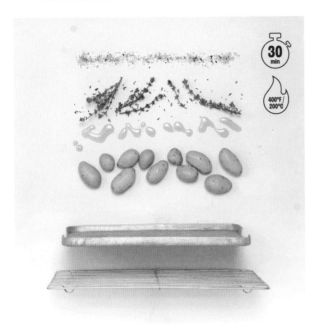

3 Make the dressing: Roughly chop the herbs and process them with the mayonnaise, yogurt, and lemon juice until smooth. Season with salt and pepper.

4 In a bowl, combine the potatoes, peas, beans, and spinach. Toss with the dressing and serve.

Grilled Cheese

4   **10 min**   **20 min**   **EQUIPMENT** 1 cutting board and 1 knife 1 skillet

INGREDIENTS

9 oz / 250 g button mushrooms

2 cloves garlic

8 sprigs parsley

8 tablespoons / 115 g unsalted butter, softened

8 large slices sandwich bread

2 cups / 200 g grated Gruyère cheese (or other Swiss-style cheese)

Salt, pepper

1 Thinly slice the mushrooms. Chop the garlic and parsley.

2 In a skillet over medium heat, melt 4 tablespoons / 60 g of the butter. Sauté the garlic, salt, pepper, and mushrooms for 5 to 10 minutes. Remove from the heat.

3 Spread one side of each slice of bread with a little of the remaining butter. Cover with the parsley, grated cheese, and mushrooms. Top with more grated cheese and parsley.

Don't forget to close the sandwiches!

4 In a skillet over low heat, cook the sandwiches for 10 minutes. Flip and cook for another 2 minutes.

Freshly baked sandwich bread from a local bakery is of much better quality. It lends a nice softness to the sandwich.

Oven-Roasted Cauliflower

INGREDIENTS

1 cauliflower (about 2 lb / 900 g)
2 cloves garlic
1 bunch cilantro
Scant ½ cup / 100 ml olive oil
1 teaspoon curry
½ teaspoon ground turmeric
1 pinch chile flakes
½ teaspoon ground coriander
Salt, pepper

4   10 min   1 hr 45 min

EQUIPMENT
1 cutting board and 1 knife
1 dutch oven

1 Remove the leaves from the cauliflower and score an x into the stem. Chop the garlic and cilantro.

2 Place the cauliflower in a pot, brush with the oil, and cover. Bake at 350°F / 180°C for 1 hour.

3 In a bowl, combine the garlic, curry, turmeric, chile flakes, and coriander. Season with salt and pepper.

4 Cover the cauliflower with the spice mixture. Bake, uncovered, for another 45 minutes. Serve with the chopped cilantro.

Once cooked, you can serve the cauliflower in wedges on a bed of hummus or labneh, with raw vegetables and chopped fresh herbs.

3-Bean Minestrone

4 | **10 min** | **45 min** | EQUIPMENT: 1 cutting board and 1 knife / 1 dutch oven

INGREDIENTS

- 2 carrots
- 1 onion
- 1 celery stalk
- 2 tomatoes
- 2 tablespoons olive oil
- ⅔ cup / 100 g canned large white beans (such as Cannellini), drained
- ⅔ cup / 100 g canned cranberry beans, drained
- 5¼ oz / 150 g fresh string beans
- 1 cube vegetable stock
- 2 oz / 60 g short pasta
- 3½ oz / 100 g baby spinach
- Salt, pepper

1 Peel the carrots and onions, and dice the carrots, onions, celery, and tomatoes. Remove the stems from the string beans and cut the beans into ¾-inch / 2 cm long sections.

2 In a dutch oven over medium heat, heat the oil, and sauté the carrots, onion, and celery for 3 minutes.

3 Add the tomatoes, beans, stock cube, and 8 cups / 2 L water. Season with salt and pepper, cover, and cook at a low boil for 20 minutes.

4 Add the pasta and spinach. Continue cooking for the time indicated on the pasta package.

In winter, replace the string beans with canned peeled tomatoes.

Soups

2-4 | 10 min | 30 min

EQUIPMENT
1 cutting board and 1 knife
1 immersion blender
1 baking sheet

VARIATIONS

Avocado-Spinach

2 avocados • 8 oz / 225 g baby spinach • 2 shallots • 2 spring onions
3½ tablespoons / 50 g lightly salted butter • Salt, pepper

Using a spoon, scrape out the flesh of the avocados and set aside. Wash the spinach. Peel and thinly slice the shallots and onions. In a saucepan over medium heat, melt the butter and sauté the shallots for 3 minutes. Add the spinach and 3⅓ cups / 800 ml water. Cover, and cook for 10 minutes. Add the avocado flesh. Using an immersion blender, blend the soup in the saucepan until smooth. Season with salt and pepper. Divide among four bowls and top with the sliced onions.

Roasted Peppers & Tomatoes

2 red bell peppers • 1 chile pepper (optional), seeded • 2 red onions, peeled
10½ oz / 300 g tomatoes • ¼ cup / 60 ml olive oil • ½ teaspoon thyme
2 oz / 60 g stale bread • ½ cube vegetable stock • Juice of ½ lime
Salt, pepper

Cut the peppers and the chile, if using, into cubes. Cut the onions and tomatoes into quarters. Place the peppers, chile, onions, and tomatoes on a baking sheet, drizzle with the oil, and sprinkle with the thyme. Season with salt and pepper. Bake at 400°F / 200°C for 25 minutes. Dissolve the stock cube in 2 cups / 480 ml hot water. Using an immersion blender, blend together the roasted vegetables, bread, stock, and lime juice. Season with salt and pepper.

Corn Chowder

1 cup / 160 g canned corn + 4 tablespoons / 40 g, for serving
7 oz / 200 g potatoes • 1 small leek • 3 cloves garlic • 5 stems chives
2 cups / 480 ml milk • 2 tablespoons unsalted butter • Salt, pepper

Drain the corn and set aside 4 tablespoons / 50 g. Peel the potatoes and cut them into cubes. Thinly slice the leek whites and halve the garlic. Finely chop the chives. In a saucepan, melt the butter over medium heat and sauté the garlic and leeks for 3 minutes. Add the potatoes and corn, cover with the milk, and season with salt and pepper. Cook for 25 minutes. Stir in 1¼ cups / 300 ml hot water (for a thinner consistency) and divide among four bowls. Before serving, top with the reserved corn and chives.

A chowder is a blended soup thickened with potato.

Golden Soup

7 oz / 200 g sweet potatoes • 10½ oz / 300 g squash
2 carrots • 1 shallot • 2 cloves garlic • 2 tablespoons sunflower oil • 1 teaspoon ground turmeric • ½ teaspoon ground ginger • 1⅔ cups / 400 ml coconut milk • 1 pinch paprika or chile powder • Salt, pepper

Peel the sweet potatoes, squash, and carrots and cut into large pieces. Thinly slice the shallot and halve the garlic. In a saucepan over medium heat, heat the oil and sauté the shallot and garlic for 2 minutes. Add the potatoes, squash, carrots, turmeric, and ginger. Cover with water and season with salt and pepper. Cover, and cook for 25 minutes. Drain, reserving the cooking liquid. Using an immersion blender, blend the vegetables with the coconut milk (reserve a few tablespoons for serving). Adjust the texture of the soup by adding a little of the reserved cooking liquid. Just before serving, drizzle with the reserved coconut milk and sprinkle with the paprika.

Hasselback Butternut Squash

👤 **6**

🥣 **10 min**

🕐 **55 min**

EQUIPMENT
1 cutting board and 1 knife
1 basting brush
2 chopsticks or small wooden dowels
1 baking sheet

INGREDIENTS

1 butternut squash

3½ tablespoons / 55 g unsalted butter, melted

Maple syrup or honey

1 teaspoon ground coriander (or other spice of your choice)

2¾ oz / 80 g feta cheese

½ cup / 50 g pomegranate seeds

⅓ cup / 50 g pumpkin seeds

4 stems chives, chopped

Salt, pepper

1 Peel the squash, cut it in half, and scrape out the seeds. Place the halves on a cutting board and place chopsticks on either side. Cut down to the chopsticks, spacing the slices ¼ inch / 5 mm apart.

2 Brush the halves with the melted butter and place the flat sides down on a parchment paper-lined baking sheet. Season with salt and pepper. Bake at 400°F / 200°C for 40 minutes.

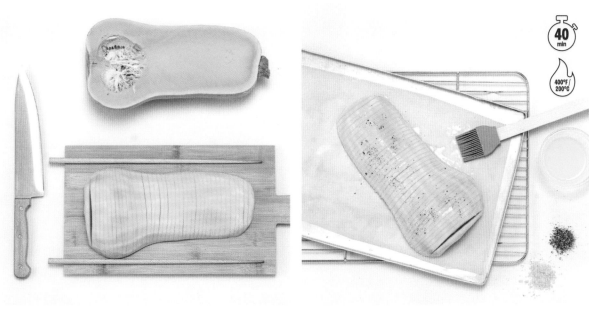

3 Brush the squash with maple syrup, sprinkle with the coriander, and bake for another 15 minutes, or until tender.

4 Remove from the oven and top with the crumbled feta and pumpkin and pomegranate seeds. Sprinkle with the chives.

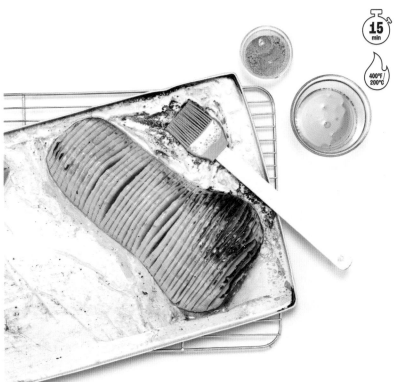

Greek Salad

4 **15 min**

EQUIPMENT
1 cutting board and 1 knife
1 citrus press

INGREDIENTS

6 heirloom tomatoes, assorted colors
9 oz / 250 g watermelon
½ cucumber
½ red onion
⅓ cup / 50 g pitted black olives
5¼ oz / 150 g feta cheese

For the dressing
Juice of ½ lemon
1 pinch dried oregano
Flaky sea salt
Pepper
⅓ cup / 80 ml olive oil

1 Cut the tomatoes into wedges, the watermelon into cubes, the cucumber into rounds, and the onion into very thin slices.

2 Make the dressing: In a small bowl, thoroughly combine the lemon juice, oregano, salt, pepper, and oil.

3

In a bowl, combine the tomatoes, watermelon, cucumber, onion, olives, crumbled feta, and dressing.

Super Simple Salads

Pasta Salad with Candied Roasted Tomatoes

4 **10 min** **20 min**

1 lb 2 oz / 500 g cherry tomatoes • Olive oil • 2 tablespoons sugar • 1 teaspoon dried oregano • ⅓ cup / 50 g pine nuts • 7 oz / 200 g short pasta (fusilli, penne, farfalle...) 3½ oz / 100 g arugula • ⅓ cup / 60 g black olives • Juice of ½ lemon • A few basil leaves Salt, pepper

Wash the tomatoes and arrange them on a parchment paper-lined baking sheet. Drizzle with 2 tablespoons oil, and sprinkle with the sugar and oregano. Season with salt and pepper. Add the pine nuts and bake at 300°F / 150°C for 20 minutes.
Cook the pasta al dente in a pot of boiling, salted water for the time indicated on the package. Drain, cool under cold running water, and coat with 1 tablespoon oil.
Combine the candied tomatoes, pine nuts, pasta, arugula, olives, lemon juice, and 1 tablespoon oil in a bowl. Season with salt and pepper, and stir to combine. Add a few basil leaves.

Change it up by replacing the pasta with white beans or chickpeas, for example.

Smashed Cucumber Salad

4   10 min   15 min

2 cucumbers • ½ teaspoon salt

Dressing
¼ bunch cilantro • 1 clove garlic • ¼ cup / 60 ml sesame oil • 1 tablespoon soy sauce
1 tablespoon sugar • 2 tablespoons apple cider vinegar • 2 tablespoons chili oil

Wash the cucumbers and cut off the ends. Crush the cucumbers by pressing them with a rolling pin. Once they are completely split lengthwise, cut them diagonally approximately every ¾ inch / 2 cm. Toss with the salt and set aside on a plate for 15 minutes.
Make the dressing: Chop the cilantro and garlic. Combine them with the sesame oil, soy sauce, sugar, vinegar, and chili oil. Drain the cucumbers by squeezing them with your hands. Combine with the dressing. Serve chilled.

You can add 2 tablespoons crushed peanuts and 2 tablespoons peanut butter to the sauce.

Mushroom Polenta

4 **10 min** **20 min**

EQUIPMENT
1 cutting board and 1 knife
1 skillet
1 saucepan

INGREDIENTS

14 oz / 400 g button mushrooms
2 cloves garlic
1 shallot
½ bunch parsley
5½ tablespoons / 85 g
unsalted butter
Scant 2 cups / 450 ml cream
4 cups / 1 L milk
⅓ oz / 10 g dried mushrooms
(porcini, morels…)
1 sprig thyme
8½ oz / 240 g precooked polenta
½ cup / 60 g grated
Parmesan cheese
Salt, pepper

1 Clean and slice the button mushrooms. Peel and chop the garlic and shallot. Chop the parsley.

2 In a skillet over high heat, melt 3½ tablespoons / 55 g of the butter and sauté the garlic, shallot, and button mushrooms for about 10 minutes. Add 1 cup / 240 ml of the cream and the parsley.

3 In a saucepan, heat the milk, remaining cream, dried mushrooms, and thyme until simmering.

4 Sprinkle in the polenta and cook for 5 minutes, stirring constantly. Stir in the remaining butter and the Parmesan. Serve with the dried mushrooms in cream.

Season with salt

Tomato Tatin

 6

 10 min

 45 min

EQUIPMENT
1 cutting board and 1 knife
1 saucepan
1 pie dish
1 skillet

INGREDIENTS

3 onions

3½ tablespoons / 55 g unsalted butter

¼ cup plus 2 tablespoons / 80 g sugar

1 Flaky Pastry (page 16), rolled out

12 oz / 350 g cherry tomatoes

Basil, for garnish

1 Peel and thinly slice the onions.

2 In a skillet over medium heat, melt the butter and sauté the onions for 3 minutes to brown them. Add 2 tablespoons of the sugar and cook for another 10 minutes.

13 min

MEDIUM HEAT

3 Place the remaining sugar in the bottom of an ovenproof pie or tart dish. Place under the broiler for 5 minutes, or until the sugar caramelizes. Remove from the oven and add the tomatoes and cooked onions to the dish.

4 Cover with the flaky pastry and tuck in the edges. Convection bake at 400°F / 200°C for 30 minutes, or until golden. Invert onto a serving dish. Top with fresh basil.

5 min

BROILER

30 min

400°F / 200°C

Pizza & Quiche

VARIATIONS

Pesto, Asparagus & Burrata Pizza

4   10 min   15 min

5 spears green asparagus • 1 red onion • 2 tablespoons olive oil • 1 Pizza Dough (page 17) or store-bought • 5¼ oz / 150 g Pesto (page 18) • 1¾ oz / 50 g arugula 9 oz / 250 g burrata • Salt, pepper

Thinly slice the asparagus lengthwise. Peel the onion and cut it into thin strips. Combine the asparagus and onion in a bowl with the oil. Season with salt and pepper. Spread the pizza dough out onto a baking sheet and spread the pesto on top. Distribute the asparagus and onion over the pesto. Bake at 475°F / 250°C on the upper rack for 10 to 15 minutes, keeping a close eye on the pizza while baking. Remove from the oven and add the arugula and drained burrata.

> **Vary the toppings and sauces, such as the roasted cherry tomatoes (page 56), Pesto (page 18), and tomato sauce (page 95).**

Squash, Spinach & Comté Quiche

4   **15 min**   **1 hr 10 min**

1 lb 11 oz / 750 g (about ½) red kuri squash (or sugar pumpkin) • Olive oil • 1 Flaky Pastry (page 16) or store-bought • 3 oz / 80 g baby spinach, or 5¼ oz / 150 g frozen spinach leaves 2 tablespoons pumpkin seeds • 4 large / 200 g eggs • 1⅔ cups / 400 ml heavy whipping cream • 1 pinch nutmeg • ½ cup / 50 g grated Comté cheese (or other grated cheese) Salt, pepper

Wash and deseed the squash. Cut into cubes and place it on a parchment-lined baking sheet. Drizzle with oil, season with salt and pepper, and bake at 400°F / 200°C for 30 minutes. Spread the dough out into a pie dish lined with parchment paper or greased and dusted with flour. Distribute the spinach, roasted squash, and pumpkin seeds on top. In a bowl, whisk together the eggs and cream. Add the nutmeg and cheese and season with salt and pepper. Pour the cream mixture over the toppings and bake at 400°F / 200°C for 45 minutes, or until golden.

Lentil Salad

4   10 min   25 min

EQUIPMENT
1 cutting board and 1 knife
1 saucepan
1 whisk

INGREDIENTS

3½ oz / 100 g cucumber (1 medium)
½ red onion
1 bunch green asparagus
¼ bunch dill
½ bunch chives
3½ oz / 100 g stale sandwich bread
¼ cup / 60 ml olive oil
1 cup / 200 g green lentils
4 large eggs
3½ oz / 100 g feta cheese
Coarse salt

Vinaigrette

1 tablespoon grainy mustard
3 tablespoons / 45 ml apple cider vinegar
¼ cup / 60 ml olive oil
Salt, pepper

25 min

MEDIUM HEAT

1

Scrape out the seeds of the cucumber and dice the flesh. Peel and thinly slice the onion. Cut the asparagus into sections. Chop the dill and chives. Cut the bread into cubes.

2

Add the lentils to a saucepan of boiling, unsalted water and cook for about 25 minutes. Drain, and cool under cool running water.

3

Cook the asparagus for 5 minutes in a separate saucepan of boiling, salted water, then immerse them in a bowl of cold water to cool.

5 min

MEDIUM HEAT

4

Cook the eggs for 6 minutes in a saucepan of boiling water, then immerse them in a bowl of cold water to cool.

6 min

MEDIUM HEAT

5

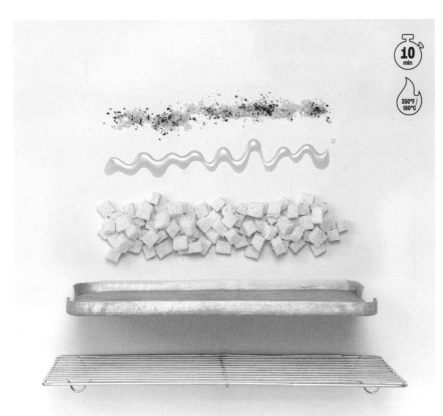

⏱ **10 min**

🔥 **350°F / 180°C**

Place the bread cubes on a baking sheet, drizzle with the olive oil, and season with salt and pepper. Bake at 350°F / 180°C for about 10 minutes.

6

In a bowl, combine the lentils, asparagus, toasted bread cubes, crumbled feta, cucumber, herbs, onion, and vinaigrette. Peel and halve the eggs and add one half to each plate.

Make the vinaigrette: Combine the mustard, vinegar, oil, and seasoning, and serve on the side!

Veggie Burger

 4

 20 min

 6 min

EQUIPMENT
1 cutting board and 1 knife
1 whisk
1 strainer
1 food processor
1 skillet

INGREDIENTS

3½ oz / 100 g carrot (1 medium)

3½ oz / 100 g red cabbage (quarter of 1 head)

½ bunch cilantro

1 avocado

4 slices Comté cheese (or other melting cheese)

2 tablespoons sunflower oil

4 hamburger buns

Salt, pepper

For the patties

3¼ oz / 90 g rustic bread

9 oz / 250 g button mushrooms

¾ cup / 120 g canned kidney beans

A small handful of cilantro, roughly chopped

1 teaspoon ground cumin

For the sauce

3 tablespoons / 40 g Mayonnaise (page 19)

1 tablespoon barbecue sauce

1 tablespoon hot sauce (Sriracha)

1

Peel and grate the carrot. Grate the cabbage. Remove the cilantro leaves from their stems. Thinly slice the avocado flesh. Begin the patties: Cut the bread into cubes and slice the mushrooms.

2

Make the sauce: Combine the mayonnaise, barbecue sauce, and hot sauce.

3

Finish the patties:
In a food processor,
process the cubed
bread, mushrooms,
drained beans,
cilantro, and cumin.
Season with salt
and pepper.

4

Dampen your hands,
and form patties
1¼-inch / 3 cm thick
and about 4 inches /
10 cm in diameter.
Place a slice of
cheese on top.

5

In a skillet over
medium heat, heat
the oil and cook the
patties for about
6 minutes.

6

Spread the sauce on the buns. Arrange the avocado slices, patty, grated carrots and cabbage, and cilantro leaves on top. Close the burgers.

Toast the buns before assembling the burgers!

Serve the burgers with sweet potato fries: Cut 1 sweet potato into thick sticks, brush with oil, season with salt and pepper, and add a pinch of cinnamon. Bake at 400°F / 200°C for 30 minutes.

Falafel

4-6   **20 min**   **25 min**

EQUIPMENT
1 cutting board and 1 knife
1 food processor
1 baking sheet

INGREDIENTS

1 cup / 200 g dried chickpeas
1 bunch parsley
½ bunch cilantro
1 spring onion
2 cloves garlic
1 teaspoon ground cumin
Juice of ½ lemon
1½ tablespoons cornstarch
½ teaspoon baking soda
Olive oil
Salt, pepper

1 The day before, soak the chickpeas in a large volume of cold water and set aside overnight.

2 Coarsely chop the parsley and cilantro. Peel and chop the onion and garlic.

3 Drain the chickpeas. In a food processor, process the chickpeas with the herbs, onion, garlic, cumin, lemon juice, cornstarch, and baking soda. Season with salt and pepper.

4 With slightly damp hands, form 1½ to 2-inch / 4 to 5 cm balls. Place the falafel on a parchment paper-lined baking sheet and drizzle with oil. Bake at 400°F / 200°C for 25 minutes.

25 min

400°F / 200°C

Serve the falafel with Roasted Carrot Hummus (page 23)

Dumplings

VARIATIONS

Ricotta-Basil

4 — 10 min — 35 min

2 cups / 480 g ricotta • 1 bunch basil • 1 cup / 100 g fine dried breadcrumbs • 1 cup / 100 g grated pecorino cheese • 1 large / 50 g egg 1 cup / 240 ml tomato sauce • Olive oil Salt, pepper

Drain the ricotta in a fine-mesh strainer. Chop the basil. In a bowl, combine the ricotta, basil, breadcrumbs, pecorino, egg, and 2 tablespoons of oil to a compact paste. Form about twenty balls. Arrange them in a casserole dish filled with the tomato sauce. Brush with oil, and season with salt and pepper. Bake at 400°F / 200°C for 35 minutes.

Red Lentil, Sweet Potato & Quinoa

4 — 10 min — 50 min

1¾ oz / 50 g sweet potato • 2 cloves garlic • ½ onion • ½ cup / 100 g red lentils 3 tablespoons / 30 g quinoa (or bulgur) • 1 teaspoon ground fenugreek ½ bunch chives • ⅔ cup / 65 g fine breadcrumbs • Olive oil • Salt, pepper

Peel the sweet potato and cut it into cubes. Peel and chop the garlic and onion. Chop the chives. In a saucepan, heat 2 tablespoons of oil over medium heat and sauté the garlic and onion for 2 minutes. Add the lentils, sweet potato, and quinoa. Add 1½ cups / 350 ml water, bring to the boil, cover, and cook for 15 minutes. Remove the lid and cook for another 10 minutes, or until all the water has evaporated. Add the fenugreek, chives, and breadcrumbs. Season with salt and pepper. Set aside for 30 minutes to cool, then form about twenty balls and place them on a parchment paper–lined baking sheet. Brush with oil. Bake at 400°F / 200°C for 20 minutes.

Broccoli & Cheddar

 4   10 min   40 min

1 lb 2 oz / 500 g broccoli • 1 cup / 100 g fine breadcrumbs • 1⅓ cups / 150 g grated cheddar cheese (or other grated cheese) • 2 large / 100 g eggs • ¼ cup / 30 g flour 1 oz / 30 g fried onions • Olive oil • Salt, pepper

Cut the broccoli into florets and place them on a parchment paper-lined baking sheet. Brush with oil, season with salt and pepper, and bake at 400°F / 200°C for 20 minutes. In a food processor, process the broccoli and incorporate the breadcrumbs, cheese, eggs, flour, and onions. Mix well to obtain a compact mixture. Form about twenty balls. Place them on a parchment paper-lined baking sheet and brush with oil. Bake at 400°F / 200°C for 20 minutes.

Vegetable Tian

4 | **15 min** | **40 min**

EQUIPMENT
1 cutting board and 1 knife
1 gratin dish

INGREDIENTS

6 tomatoes
2 zucchini
2 eggplants
3 red onions
⅔ cup / 150 ml olive oil
Fresh thyme
Fresh rosemary
Ground bay leaf
Oregano
Salt, pepper

1 Cut the tomatoes, zucchini, eggplants, and onions into thin rounds of about ⅛-inch / 3 mm thick.

2 In a gratin dish, arrange the slices in a single layer, alternating them, and fitting them in snuggly. Season with salt and pepper, and sprinkle on the herbs.

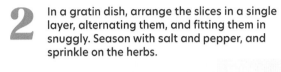

40 min

350°F / 180°C

3

Drizzle with the oil.
Bake at 350°F /180°C for 40 minutes.

Vegetarian Chili

 4

 10 min

 30 min

EQUIPMENT 1 cutting board and 1 knife
1 dutch oven

INGREDIENTS

1 onion
3 cloves garlic
2 red bell peppers
1 carrot
2 tablespoons sunflower oil
2 teaspoons Mexican blend seasoning
8 oz / 225 g chopped tomatoes
⅔ cup / 150 ml water
Just over ¾ cup / 150 g canned kidney beans
⅔ cup / 100 g canned corn

¼ cup / 60 g sour cream
½ bunch cilantro
½ lime
Chile flakes
Salt, pepper

1 Peel and chop the onion and garlic. Cut the peppers into strips. Peel the carrot and cut it into small cubes.

2 In a dutch oven over medium heat, heat the oil and sauté the onion, garlic, and carrot for 2 minutes. Add the peppers and cook for another 3 minutes.

3 Add the seasoning blend, tomatoes, and water. Season with salt and pepper. Cover, and simmer for 20 minutes over medium heat, stirring occasionally.

4 Add the drained beans and corn. Continue cooking for 5 minutes.

Serve each bowl with a dollop of sour cream, chopped cilantro leaves, a few lime wedges, and a few chile flakes.

Green Shakshuka

👤 4

🥣 15 min

🕐 35 min

EQUIPMENT
1 cutting board and 1 knife
1 skillet
1 food processor

INGREDIENTS

3 leeks
½ fennel bulb
1 zucchini
3 cloves garlic
5 sprigs parsley
3½ tablespoons / 55 g unsalted butter, melted
2¾ oz / 80 g baby spinach
2 tablespoons heavy whipping cream
½ cup / 120 g Greek yogurt
4 large eggs
1 loaf rustic bread
Salt, pepper

1

Rinse the leeks and cut them into small pieces. Slice the fennel. Peel and dice the zucchini. Chop the garlic and parsley.

2

Over medium heat, sauté the chopped garlic, leeks, and fennel in the butter for 10 minutes.

3

Add the zucchini and
⅔ cup / 150 ml water.
Season with salt and
pepper. Cover, and
cook for 15 minutes
over medium heat.

4

Remove the lid and
check the doneness
of the vegetables.
Once cooked, process
a third of the mixture
in a food processor
with the spinach,
cream, and yogurt.

5

Pour the mixture into the
skillet, stir, and make four
hollows using the back
of a spoon.

6

Crack the eggs directly into
each hollow. Cover, and
cook over very low heat for
5 to 10 minutes. Just before
serving, add the chopped
parsley along with a few
slices of rustic bread on
the side.

**For a classic red
shakshuka, replace
the vegetables with
2 red bell peppers,
1 lb 8 oz / 700 g tomatoes,
and 2 onions. Add
1 tablespoon sugar,
1 teaspoon cumin, and
1 teaspoon smoked
paprika during cooking.**

Veggie Ramen

 4

 10 min

 20 min

EQUIPMENT
1 cutting board and 1 knife
1 dutch oven
1 saucepan
4 large bowls

INGREDIENTS

1 carrot

1¼-inch / 3 cm piece fresh ginger

2 scallions

1 tablespoon sunflower oil

3 cloves garlic

¼ cup plus 2 tablespoons / 90 ml soy sauce

1 cube vegetable stock

4 dried shiitake mushrooms

12 oz / 350 g thick wheat noodles (such as udon)

3½ oz / 100 g baby spinach

5¼ oz / 150 g white shimeji mushrooms (or white button mushrooms)

For the Ramen Eggs (page 15)

4 large eggs

⅔ cup / 150 ml soy sauce

2 tablespoons sugar

1 Very thinly slice the carrot. Peel and finely chop the ginger. Peel and chop the garlic. Finely chop the scallions.

2 In a dutch oven over medium heat, heat the oil and sauté the garlic and ginger. Add the soy sauce, stock cube, 8 cups / 2 L water, and shiitake mushrooms. Bring to a boil, cover, and simmer for 15 minutes.

15 min

MEDIUM HEAT

3 Add the noodles to a saucepan of boiling water and cook for the time indicated on the package.

4 Divide the noodles, carrots, spinach, shiitake mushrooms, shimeji mushrooms, and scallions among four large bowls. Add a marinated egg to each bowl.

Classic Curry

4

10 min

30 min

EQUIPMENT
1 cutting board and 1 knife
1 dutch oven

INGREDIENTS

1 onion

2 cloves garlic

1½-inch / 4 cm piece
fresh ginger

12 oz / 350 g zucchini

10½ oz / 300 g carrots

7 oz / 200 g potatoes

2 tablespoons sunflower oil

2 tablespoons curry powder

1 teaspoon ground turmeric

2 tablespoons tomato paste

1 tablespoon cornstarch

1 cube
vegetable stock

⅔ cup / 100 g canned
chickpeas, drained

Just over ¾ cup /
200 ml coconut milk

A few sprigs cilantro

Salt, pepper

1 Peel and chop the onion and garlic. Grate the ginger. Cut the zucchini and carrots into thick rounds and the potatoes into large pieces.

2 In a dutch oven over medium heat, heat the oil and sauté the onion, garlic, ginger, curry, and turmeric for 3 minutes.

3 min

MEDIUM HEAT

3 Add the potatoes, carrots, tomato paste, and cornstarch. Stir. Add 2 cups / 480 ml water and the stock cube. Bring to a boil, cover, and cook over medium heat for 20 minutes.

20 min

MEDIUM HEAT

4 Add the zucchini, chickpeas, and coconut milk. Cook over medium heat, uncovered, for 10 minutes. Season with salt and pepper. Serve with rice sprinkled with chopped cilantro.

10 min

LOW HEAT

Curries of the World

Thai Curry

VARIATIONS

4   10 min   20 min

1 lemongrass stalk • 1 shallot • 1¼-inch / 3 cm piece fresh ginger, peeled • 1 small Thai chile pepper (optional) • 10½ oz / 300 g sweet potatoes • 2 tablespoons sunflower oil • 1 tablespoon green curry paste • 1 tablespoon turbinado sugar 1 pinch coarse salt • 9 oz / 250 g frozen green vegetable mix • Just over ¾ cup / 200 ml coconut milk • Juice of ½ lime 2 tablespoons soy sauce

Peel away the two outer leaves from the lemongrass. Peel the shallot. Cut the lemongrass, shallot, ginger, and chile, if using, into thin slices. Peel the potatoes and cut them into cubes. In a dutch oven over medium heat, heat the oil and sauté the lemongrass, shallot, ginger, and chile for 2 minutes. Add the curry paste and cook for 1 minute, stirring occasionally. Add the potatoes, 1⅔ cups / 400 ml water, sugar, and salt. Cover, bring to a boil, and cook for 10 minutes. Add the frozen vegetables and the coconut milk and simmer, uncovered, for another 10 minutes. Just before serving, add the lime juice and soy sauce. To flavor the curry even more, add 2 makrut lime leaves (found in Asian markets) at the beginning of the cooking time.

You can enrich this curry with 7 oz / 200 g firm, cubed tofu added with the frozen vegetables, or with a few crushed peanuts sprinkled on top before serving.

Indian-Style Korma Curry

4 | **10 min** | **35 min**

1 onion • 2 cloves garlic • 1½-inch / 4 cm piece fresh ginger • ½ head cauliflower • 1 zucchini • 9 oz / 250 g potatoes • 2 tablespoons unsalted butter • 2 tablespoons korma curry powder • 2 tablespoons tomato paste • 1 pinch coarse salt 1⅔ cups / 400 ml coconut milk ⅓ cup / 50g chopped cashews A few sprigs cilantro

Peel and chop the onion and garlic. Peel and grate the ginger. Cut the cauliflower into florets and the zucchini into rounds. Peel the potatoes and cut them into large cubes. In a dutch oven over medium heat, melt the butter and sauté the onion, garlic, and ginger for 2 minutes. Add the curry and tomato paste and combine. Add the potatoes, 1⅔ cups / 400 ml water, and salt. Cover, bring to a boil, and cook for 15 minutes. Add the cauliflower, zucchini, coconut milk, and half the cashews. Cover and cook for another 15 minutes. Serve with a few cilantro leaves and the remaining cashews on top.

To make your own korma spice blend, combine equal parts ground coriander, turmeric, cumin, ginger, salt, and garam masala.

Sweet Potato Gnocchi

INGREDIENTS

- 12 oz / 350 g sweet potatoes
- 11½ oz / 330 g yellow potatoes
- 2⅔ cups / 330 g all-purpose flour
- 2 large / 40 g egg yolks
- 3½ oz / 100 g blue cheese, crumbled
- ¼ cup / 60 ml olive oil
- ½ bunch chives
- Salt, pepper

4   **20 min**   **1 hr**

EQUIPMENT
- Aluminum foil
- 1 potato masher
- 1 knife
- 1 saucepan

1 Using the tip of a knife, prick the sweet potatoes and yellow potatoes all over. Wrap them in foil and bake at 400°F / 200°C for 1 hour.

2 Peel the potatoes. Mash the flesh using a potato masher, then combine with the flour and yolks to make a dough. Season with salt and pepper.

3 Quarter the dough. On a floured work surface using your palms, roll out ¾-inch / 2 cm thick ropes and cut them widthwise every 1¼ inches / 3 cm. Place the gnocchi on a floured baking sheet, keeping them separated to prevent sticking.

4 Cook the gnocchi in a saucepan of boiling, salted water for about 3 minutes, or until they float to the surface. Drain, and serve with the cheese, oil, and chopped chives over the top.

Vegetable Stir-Fried Rice

 4   10 min   15 min   **EQUIPMENT** 1 cutting board and 1 knife / 1 saucepan / 1 skillet

INGREDIENTS

- ½ cup / 100 g cooked white rice (such as jasmine)
- 1 onion
- 1 carrot
- 4¼ oz / 120 g Savoy cabbage
- ½ bunch cilantro
- 3 scallions
- 3 tablespoons / 45 ml sunflower oil
- 2 large eggs
- 3½ oz / 100 g bean sprouts
- 3 tablespoons / 45 ml soy sauce
- Salt, pepper

1 Cook white rice according to the instructions on the package. Drain, and set aside the quantity needed.

2 Peel and chop the onion. Cut the carrot into small cubes. Cut the cabbage into thin strips. Chop the cilantro and scallions.

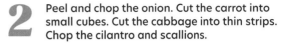

3 In a skillet over high heat, heat the oil and sauté the onion and carrot for 3 minutes. Add the cabbage, season with salt and pepper, and cook for another 2 minutes.

4 Group the vegetables on one side of the pan and crack the eggs into the center of the pan. Stir to scramble and combine with the vegetables. Add the cooked rice, cilantro, scallions, sprouts, and soy sauce, to taste. Stir to combine and continue cooking for 3 minutes.

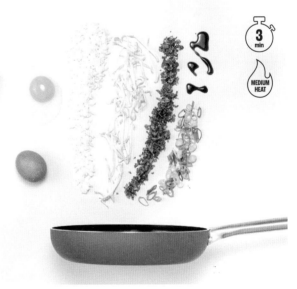

This recipe works even better using rice cooked the night before!

Eggplant Parmesan

4-6

10 min

50 min

EQUIPMENT
1 cutting board and 1 knife
1 baking sheet
1 dutch oven
1 casserole dish

INGREDIENTS

4 eggplants
2 cloves garlic
1 onion
1 bunch basil
9 oz / 250 g mozzarella
2½ cups / 600 ml tomato purée
½ cup / 60 g grated
Parmesan cheese
Olive oil
Salt, pepper

1 Cut the eggplants lengthwise into about ¼-inch / 0.5 cm thick slices. Peel and chop the garlic and onion. Chop the basil. Slice the mozzarella.

2 Place the eggplants on a baking sheet, brush with oil, and season with salt and pepper. Bake at 400°F / 200°C for 20 minutes.

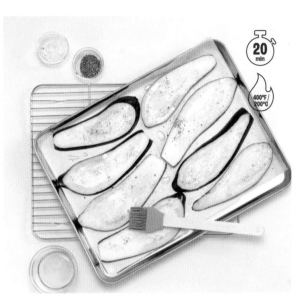

3 In a dutch oven over medium heat, heat 3 tablespoons / 45 ml oil and sauté the garlic and onion for 2 minutes. Add the tomato sauce and basil. Season with salt and pepper, cover, and cook for 15 minutes.

4 Cover the bottom of a casserole dish with eggplant slices and spread the sauce, mozzarella, and Parmesan over the top. Repeat until all the ingredients are used. Bake at 400°F / 200°C for 25 minutes.

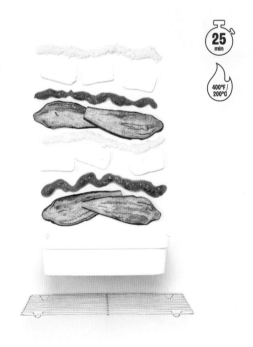

Spring Tabbouleh

4 | **10 min** | **11 min**

EQUIPMENT
1 cutting board and 1 knife
1 saucepan

INGREDIENTS

1 cup / 150 g bulgur
7 oz / 200 g frozen peas
1 bunch dill
1 bunch chives
1 scallion
1 cucumber
1 bunch radishes, assorted colors
1 avocado

Sauce
Juice of 1 lemon
⅓ cup / 80 ml olive oil
1 teaspoon ground cumin
Salt, pepper

1 In a saucepan of boiling, salted water, cook the bulgur for 6 minutes. Add the peas and cook for 5 minutes. Drain.

2 Chop the dill and chives. Thinly slice the scallion, cucumber, radishes, and avocado flesh.

11 min

MEDIUM HEAT

3 Make the dressing: Combine the lemon juice, oil, and cumin. Season with salt and pepper.

4 In a bowl, combine the cooked bulgur and peas, dill, chives, scallion, cucumber, radishes, and avocado. Add the dressing and stir to coat.

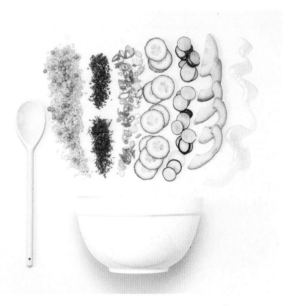

You can enrich the recipe by adding pomegranate seeds and a little crumbled feta.

Carrot & Lentil Dal

4   **10 min**   **15 min**

EQUIPMENT 1 cutting board and 1 knife
1 dutch oven

INGREDIENTS

1 carrot

1 zucchini

1 tomato

1 onion

2 cloves garlic

1¼-inch / 3 cm piece fresh ginger

¾ cup / 150 g red lentils

1 cube vegetable stock

1 teaspoon ground turmeric

1 teaspoon ground cumin

1¾ oz / 50 g baby spinach

Just over ¾ cup / 200 ml coconut milk

A few sprigs cilantro

1 Very thinly slice the carrot and zucchini. Chop the tomato. Peel and chop the onion, garlic, and ginger.

2 In a dutch oven over medium heat, sauté the onion, garlic, and ginger for 2 minutes.

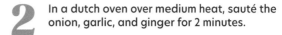

3 Add the carrots, tomatoes, lentils, stock cube, turmeric, and cumin. Stir to combine. Cook, covered, over medium heat for 10 minutes.

4 Add the zucchini, spinach, and coconut milk. Continue cooking for 3 to 5 minutes. Just before serving, top with cilantro sprigs.

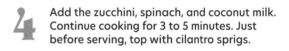

Dal originates from India and is made with red lentils and spices, but you can vary the types of lentils. Accompany with rice or vegetables. The dish is delicious with Oven-Roasted Cauliflower (page 46)!

Pasta with Leeks

 4   **10 min**   **15 min**

EQUIPMENT
1 cutting board and 1 knife
1 saucepan
1 skillet

INGREDIENTS
14 oz / 400 g leeks
3 cloves garlic
2 tablespoons unsalted butter
10½ oz / 300 g long pasta (linguine, spaghetti, tagliatelle...)
2 tablespoons ground black pepper
1 cup / 100 g grated pecorino cheese
Salt

1 Cut off the rough ends of the leek greens. Slice the leeks lengthwise, rinse any dirt from between the leaves, and finely chop. Peel and chop the garlic.

2 In a skillet over medium heat, melt the butter and add the leeks. Cover and cook for 10 to 12 minutes. Season with salt and pepper.

12 min

MEDIUM HEAT

3 In a pot of boiling, salted water, cook the pasta for the time indicated on the package. Reserve ⅔ cup / 150 ml of the pasta cooking water. Drain.

4 Add the garlic, pepper, and reserved pasta water to the skillet. Add the pecorino and let melt for about 1 minute without stirring. Stir, and add the cooked pasta.

Risotto Verde

4   10 min   20 min

EQUIPMENT
1 cutting board and 1 knife
1 dutch oven
1 food processor

INGREDIENTS

2 shallots

2 cloves garlic

3½ tablespoons / 55 g unsalted butter

1 cup / 200 g arborio rice

Scant ½ cup / 100 ml dry white wine

2 stock cubes, dissolved in 4 ½ cups / 1L hot water

3½ oz / 100 g baby spinach

4 sprigs basil

¼ cup / 30 g grated Parmesan cheese

3 tablespoons / 45 ml crème fraîche

Salt, pepper

1

3 min

MEDIUM HEAT

Peel and chop the shallots and garlic.

2

In a dutch oven over medium heat, melt the butter and sauté the shallots and garlic for 2 minutes. Add the rice, stir, and continue cooking for 1 minute until the rice is translucent.

3

Add the wine and stir gently to combine.

4

Cook over medium heat while gradually adding the hot stock, stirring frequently. Add more stock as soon as the rice has absorbed each addition.

5

In a food processor, process the spinach, basil, Parmesan, and crème fraîche. Season with salt and pepper.

6

After the rice has cooked for 20 minutes, stir in the spinach mixture and combine.

Mushroom Bourguignon

4-6 **15 min** **1 hr 30 min** **EQUIPMENT** 1 cutting board and 1 knife
1 skillet
1 dutch oven

INGREDIENTS

2 shallots

2 carrots

7 oz / 200 g smoked tofu

14 oz / 400 g assorted mushrooms
(porcini, chanterelle, black trumpet)

Scant ½ cup / 100 ml sunflower oil

8½ tablespoons / 125 g unsalted butter

2½ tablespoons / 20 g all-purpose flour

1 bottle / 750 ml red wine

Just over ¾ cup / 200 ml
vegetable stock

1 bouquet garni (parsley,
bay leaves, thyme)

2 tablespoons soy sauce

1 Peel and thinly slice the shallots. Peel and cut the carrots into rounds and the tofu into small cubes. Clean the mushrooms and quarter them.

2 In a skillet over high heat, heat the oil and start cooking some of the mushrooms with a pinch of salt and pepper. Add the remaining mushrooms in stages, cooking each addition slightly before adding the next.

3 In a dutch oven over medium heat, melt the butter. Cook the shallots, carrots, and tofu for 2 minutes.

4 Add the sautéed mushrooms and sprinkle the flour over them. Stir, then add the wine and stock. Add the bouquet garni and soy sauce. Cover, and simmer over medium heat for 1 hour 15 minutes.

3 min

MEDIUM HEAT

75 min

MEDIUM HEAT

Celery Root Milanese

4   **15 min**   **30 min**

EQUIPMENT
1 cutting board and 1 knife
1 baking sheet
1 vegetable peeler
1 skillet

INGREDIENTS

1 celery root
3 zucchini
7 oz / 200 g cherry tomatoes
1 clove garlic
½ bunch parsley
¼ cup / 60 ml olive oil
Juice of ½ lemon
2 tablespoons unsalted butter
Salt, pepper

For the breading
⅔ cup / 65 g breadcrumbs
½ cup / 60 g grated Parmesan cheese
1 teaspoon herbes de Provence
¼ cup plus 2 tablespoons / 50 g all-purpose flour
2 large eggs

1

⏱ **20 min**

🔥 **400°F / 200°C**

Cut the celery root into ¾-inch / 2 cm thick slices. Using a vegetable peeler, make thin long "noodles" with the zucchini. Halve the tomatoes. Chop the garlic and parsley.

2

Place the celery root slices on a parchment paper-lined baking sheet. Brush with 3 tablespoons / 45 ml of the oil, and season with salt and pepper. Bake at 400°F / 200°C for 20 minutes.

3

Combine the zucchini, garlic, lemon juice, remaining oil, parsley, and tomatoes.

4

Make the breading: In a deep bowl, combine the breadcrumbs, Parmesan, and herbes de Provence. Season with salt and pepper.

*Breaded
celery root steaks!*

5

Spread the flour out onto a plate. Lightly beat the eggs on a separate plate. Dredge the celery slices in the flour on both sides, then in the egg, then on both sides in the breadcrumb mixture.

6

In a skillet over medium heat, melt the butter. Cook the slices for 3 minutes on each side to brown. Serve with the zucchini "noodles" on the side.

Vegetarian Couscous

 6

 10 min

 50 min

EQUIPMENT: 1 cutting board and 1 knife
1 dutch oven

INGREDIENTS

4 small potatoes

4 carrots

6 baby turnips

3 zucchini

1 onion

2 cloves garlic

8 sprigs cilantro, plus more for the couscous

2 tablespoons olive oil, plus more for the couscous

½ teaspoon cinnamon

2 tablespoons ras el hanout spice blend

1 teaspoon harissa (optional)

1 cup / 160 g canned chickpeas, drained

6 dried apricots (or 2 tablespoons raisins)

1¼ cups / 240 g medium-grain couscous

Kosher salt

1 Peel the potatoes (cut them in half if they are large). Peel and slice the carrots. Cut the tops off the turnips. Cut the zucchini into large pieces. Peel and chop the onion and garlic. Chop the cilantro.

2 In a dutch oven over medium heat, heat the oil and sauté the onion and garlic with the cinnamon, ras el hanout, and harissa, if using, for 3 minutes.

3 Add the carrots, turnips, and potatoes. Sauté for several minutes. Add 4 cups / 1 L water and season with salt. Bring to a boil, cover, and cook for 30 minutes.

4 Add the zucchini, chickpeas, and apricots. Cover, and cook for another 15 minutes.

Prepare the couscous by covering it with 1¼ cups / 300 ml boiling, salted water. Let swell, then fluff with a fork and combine with a little olive oil and chopped cilantro.

Lentil Shepherd's Pie

6   **15 min**   **55 min**

EQUIPMENT
1 cutting board and 1 knife
1 dutch oven
1 potato masher
1 skillet
1 casserole dish

INGREDIENTS

2 small carrots
1 lb 2 oz / 500 g sweet potatoes
2 shallots
2 cloves garlic
6 sprigs parsley
2 tablespoons sunflower oil
1¼ cups / 250 g green lentils
9 oz / 250 g tomato purée
1 cube vegetable stock
6 tablespoons / 90 g butter
3 tablespoons / 20 g breadcrumbs

3 tablespoons / 20 g grated pecorino cheese (or other cheese of your choice)

Salt, pepper

1

⏱ **3 min**

🔥 **MEDIUM HEAT**

Peel and finely dice the carrots. Peel the sweet potato and cut it into large pieces. Peel and finely chop the shallots and garlic. Chop the parsley.

2

In a dutch oven over medium heat, heat the oil and sauté the shallots, garlic, and carrots with a pinch of salt and pepper for about 3 minutes.

3

Add the lentils, tomato sauce, stock cube, and 2 cups / 480 ml water. Bring to a boil, cover, and cook over medium heat for 25 minutes.

25 min

MEDIUM HEAT

4

In a saucepan of boiling, salted water, cook the sweet potatoes for about 15 minutes.

15 min

MEDIUM HEAT

5

Drain the sweet potatoes, and mash them with 4 tablespoons / 60 g of the butter and a little pepper.

In a casserole dish, add the lentil mixture, then cover evenly with the sweet potatoes. Sprinkle the breadcrumbs and pecorino on top.
Distribute the remaining butter on top.
Place under the broiler on low for 25 minutes, or until lightly browned.

Tex-Mex Stuffed Bell Peppers

 4

 10 min

 35 min

EQUIPMENT 1 cutting board and 1 knife
1 baking sheet

INGREDIENTS

4 red bell peppers
2 scallions
3½ oz / 100 g cherry tomatoes
2 cloves garlic
1 bunch parsley
7 oz / 200 g tofu
1 teaspoon Mexican spice blend
1 teaspoon smoked paprika
½ cup / 80 g canned corn, drained
½ cup / 80 g canned kidney beans, drained
¾ cup / 90 g grated cheddar cheese
Olive oil
Salt, pepper

1 Halve and clean out the peppers. Thinly slice the scallions and quarter the tomatoes. Peel and chop the garlic. Chop the parsley. Crumble the tofu.

2 Place the peppers on a parchment paper-lined baking sheet, hollow side up. Season with salt and pepper, and drizzle with oil. Bake at 400°F / 200°C for 20 minutes.

3 In a large bowl, combine the tofu, onions, garlic, tomatoes, parsley, spice blend, paprika, corn, beans, and cheese. Season with salt and pepper.

4 Stuff the peppers with the mixture and bake for 15 minutes.

Stuffed Vegetables

VARIATIONS

Eggplant with Goat Cheese

4   **10 min**   **30 min**

2 eggplants • 2 oz / 60 g dry bread • Just over ¾ cup / 200 ml milk • 1 shallot • 1 clove garlic • 5¼ oz / 150 g fresh goat cheese • 1 teaspoon oregano • 1 bunch chives 1 zucchini, grated • Salt, pepper

Bring a pot of water to a boil. Add the eggplants whole and boil for 10 minutes. Drain, let cool, then cut lengthwise in half and collect the flesh, leaving about ⅜ inch / 1 cm of flesh in the skin. Cut the bread into pieces and soak it in the milk. Peel and chop the shallot and garlic. Combine the shallot, garlic, bread (wrung of excess milk), eggplant flesh, cheese, and oregano. Chop the chives and grate the zucchini and incorporate them into the mixture. Season with salt and pepper. Fill the eggplant skins and bake on the upper rack at 400°F / 200°C for 20 minutes.

Loaded Sweet Potatoes with White Beans

4   10 min   1 hr

2 sweet potatoes • 1 red bell pepper • ⅔ cup / 100 g canned white beans (such as cannellini or navy), drained 1 teaspoon smoked paprika • 4 sprigs parsley, chopped 7 oz / 200 g mozzarella, roughly chopped • Olive oil Salt, pepper

Wash the sweet potatoes and prick them all over using the tip of a knife. Place them on a parchment paper-lined baking sheet. Coat with 1 tablespoon oil and season with salt and pepper. Bake at 425°F / 220°C for 45 minutes. Dice the pepper. In a casserole dish, combine the beans, pepper, and 1 tablespoon oil. Season with salt and pepper. Bake for 15 minutes. Halve the roasted potatoes. Toss the beans and bell pepper with the parsley and mozzarella. Fill the potatoes with the mixture and bake at 400°F / 200°C for 15 minutes in the upper rack, ensuring they do not brown too much.

Veggie Bolognese Pasta

4 **15 min** **30 min**

EQUIPMENT
1 cutting board and 1 knife
1 dutch oven
1 saucepan

INGREDIENTS

14 oz / 400 g button mushrooms
1 onion
2 cloves garlic
1 carrot
2 celery stalks
2 tablespoons olive oil
1 lb 12 oz / 800 g crushed tomatoes
3 tablespoons / 45 ml soy sauce
1 teaspoon dried thyme
⅓ cup / 60 g quinoa

14 oz / 400 g long pasta (linguine, spaghetti...)
⅓ cup / 40 g grated Parmesan cheese
Salt, pepper

1 Clean and chop the mushrooms. Peel and chop the onion and garlic. Peel and dice the carrot. Thinly slice the celery.

2 In a dutch oven, sauté the mushrooms, onion, garlic, carrots, and celery in the oil, stirring often. Add the tomatoes, soy sauce, thyme, quinoa, salt, pepper, and scant ½ cup / 100 ml water.

5 min

MEDIUM HEAT

3 In a saucepan of boiling, salted water, cook the pasta for the time indicated on the package.

7 min

MEDIUM HEAT

4 Drain the pasta and combine with the sauce. Serve sprinkled with the Parmesan.

To save time, chop the vegetables using a food processor.

Goat Cheese & Zucchini Casserole

4   10 min   50 min

EQUIPMENT
1 cutting board and 1 knife
1 casserole dish

INGREDIENTS

1 lb 11 oz / 750 g zucchini
2 cloves garlic
6 sprigs parsley
5¼ oz / 150 g log fresh goat cheese
3 sprigs thyme
2 tablespoons olive oil
4 large / 200 g eggs
1¼ cups / 300 ml heavy whipping cream
2¼ oz / 65 g fresh goat cheese, grated
¼ cup / 30 g all-purpose flour
1 pinch nutmeg
Salt, pepper

1 Cut the zucchini into rounds. Peel and chop the garlic. Chop the parsley. Slice the goat cheese log into thin rounds.

2 In a casserole dish, layer the zucchini, garlic, and thyme sprigs. Season with salt and pepper. Drizzle with the oil. Bake at 400°F / 200°C for 20 minutes, stirring halfway through the baking time.

3 In a large bowl, whisk together the eggs, cream, parsley, grated cheese, flour, nutmeg, salt, and pepper.

4 Place the goat cheese slices on top of the zucchini and pour in the egg mixture. Bake at 400°F / 200°C for 30 minutes, or until well browned.

Winter Squash Lasagna

 8

 20 min

 1 hr 15 min

EQUIPMENT
1 cutting board and 1 knife
1 dutch oven
1 skillet
1 saucepan
1 casserole dish

INGREDIENTS

3 cloves garlic
1 onion
1 butternut squash
½ red kuri squash (or sugar pumpkin)
12 lasagna noodles
9 oz / 250 g mushrooms of your choice
½ bunch parsley
3 tablespoons / 45 g unsalted butter
1 sprig rosemary
¼ cup plus 2 tablespoons / 90 ml olive oil
Salt, pepper

For the béchamel sauce
3 tablespoons / 45 g unsalted butter
¼ cup plus 1 tablespoon / 40 g all-purpose flour
2½ cups / 600 ml milk
1 pinch nutmeg
¾ cup / 75 g grated pecorino cheese, plus more for topping

1

Peel and chop the garlic and onion. Peel and halve the butternut squash and slice it widthwise. Cut the kuri squash into cubes with the skin on. Thinly slice the mushrooms. Chop the parsley.

17 min

MEDIUM HEAT

2

In a dutch oven over medium heat, melt half the butter and sauté the onion, kuri squash, and rosemary for 2 minutes. Season with salt and pepper, and cover with water. Cook for 15 minutes, covered.

3

Drain, reserving ⅔ cup / 150 ml of the cooking liquid. Remove the rosemary, then blend the onion, kuri squash, and reserved cooking liquid to a purée.

4

In a skillet, melt the remaining butter and sauté the garlic and mushrooms for 10 minutes, stirring occasionally.

5

Make the béchamel sauce: In a saucepan over medium heat, melt the butter and add the flour and garlic. Mix to form a paste, then stir in the milk, whisking constantly, until thickened to a coating consistency. Add the nutmeg and pecorino. Season with salt and pepper.

6

Grease a casserole dish using the oil, then add a layer of the kuri squash purée, a layer of lasagna noodles, a layer of kuri squash purée, a layer of butternut squash, a little béchamel, and all the mushrooms. Repeat these steps, finishing with a layer of béchamel. Cover with parsley and cheese. Bake at 350°F / 180°C for 45 minutes. Cover with aluminum foil, and bake for another 15 minutes.

You can omit the mushrooms to simplify the recipe.

Green Veggie Casserole

   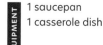

6   **15 min**   **30 min**   **EQUIPMENT**

1 saucepan
1 casserole dish

INGREDIENTS

5¼ oz / 150 g frozen broccoli
5¼ oz / 150 g frozen snow peas
7 oz / 200 g frozen peas

For the béchamel sauce

3 tablespoons / 45 g unsalted butter
¼ cup plus 1 tablespoon / 40 g all-purpose flour
2 cups / 480 ml milk
1 pinch nutmeg
Salt, pepper

For the crumble topping

5 tablespoons / 75 g unsalted butter
¾ cup / 100 g all-purpose flour
¾ cup / 75 g grated pecorino cheese

1 In a saucepan of boiling, salted water, cook the frozen broccoli, snow peas, and peas according to the instructions on the package. Drain, then transfer to a large bowl of cold water.

2 Make the béchamel sauce: In a saucepan over medium heat, melt the butter and add the flour. Mix to form a paste, then stir in the milk, whisking constantly, until thickened to a coating consistency. Add the nutmeg and season with salt and pepper.

3 Make the crumble topping: In a large bowl, combine the butter, flour, and pecorino to a sandy consistency.

4 In a casserole dish, add the cooked drained vegetables and the béchamel. Cover with the crumble topping. Bake at 400°F / 200°C for 30 minutes.

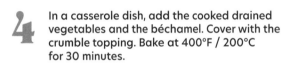

Green Waffles with Eggs

4 — **10 min** — **20 min**

EQUIPMENT
1 blender
1 waffle maker
1 cutting board and 1 knife
1 skillet

INGREDIENTS

For the waffle batter
3 large / 150 g eggs
⅔ cup / 150 ml heavy whipping cream
7 oz / 200 g baby spinach
2 oz / 60 g fresh goat cheese, grated
2 cups / 250 g all-purpose flour
1⅛ teaspoons baking powder
1 tablespoon unsalted butter
Salt, pepper

For the toppings
2 avocados
½ red onion
3½ oz / 100 g cherry tomatoes
8 large eggs
¾ cup / 200 g sour cream
Chile flakes

1

In a blender, blend the eggs, cream, spinach, cheese, flour, and baking powder until well blended. Season with salt and pepper.

2

In a greased waffle maker, pour in a little batter and cook for 5 minutes. Repeat until all the batter is used.

3

Prepare the toppings: Cut the avocado flesh into thin slices. Chop the onion. Quarter the tomatoes.

4

In a skillet over medium heat, melt the butter. Fry each egg for about 2 minutes. Season with salt and pepper.

Top each waffle with a little sour cream, avocado slices, a fried egg, onion, and tomatoes. Add a pinch of salt, pepper, and chile flakes.

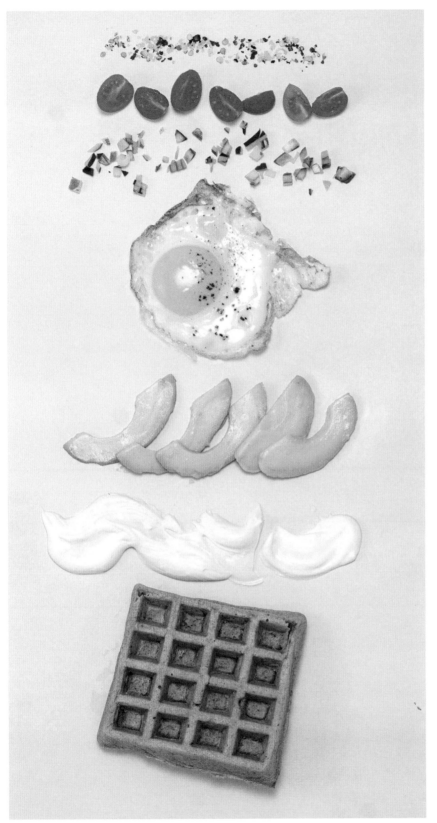

Fudgy Chocolate-Avocado Cake

INGREDIENTS

7 oz / 200 g dark chocolate
4 large / 200 g eggs
1 large ripe avocado
¼ cup plus 2 tablespoons / 80 g sugar
¾ cup / 100 g all-purpose flour
1⅛ teaspoons baking powder

 4
 5 min
 25 min

EQUIPMENT
1 saucepan
1 blender
1 baking dish

1 In a double boiler or the microwave set at 50% power, melt the chocolate, ensuring it does not get too hot.

2 In a blender, blend the eggs, avocado flesh, melted chocolate, sugar, flour, and baking powder for 30 seconds until smooth.

Don't forget to remove the pit!

20 min

350°F / 180°C

3

Grease and flour a small baking dish. Pour in the batter. Bake at 350°F / 180°C for 20 minutes, or until dulled on top and just set.

Carrot Cake

 8

 15 min

 45 min

EQUIPMENT
1 cutting board and 1 knife
1 grater
1 electric mixer
1 cake pan

INGREDIENTS

2 small carrots
2 cups / 200 g pecans
4 large / 200 g eggs
¾ packed cup / 160 g brown sugar
Scant ½ cup / 100 ml sunflower oil

1¼ cups / 155 g all-purpose flour
1⅛ teaspoons baking powder
2 pinches cinnamon
1 pinch allspice

For the icing
7 oz / 200 g crème fraîche
Juice of ¼ lemon
½ cup / 50 g confectioners' sugar

1

Peel and grate
the carrots. Coarsely chop
the pecans and set aside
½ cup / 60 g.

2

Using an electric mixer
on high speed, beat
the eggs and sugar for
3 minutes. Drizzle in the
oil while beating.

3

Add the flour, baking powder, 1 pinch cinnamon, and allspice. Stir in the carrots and the remaining pecans.

4

Scrape the batter into a greased and floured cake pan. Bake at 350°F / 180°C for about 45 minutes, or just until a toothpick inserted in the center has a few moist crumbs. Set on a cooling rack to cool completely before unmolding.

5

Make the icing: Whisk together the crème fraîche, lemon juice, and confectioners' sugar.

6 Spread the icing over the cooled cake, sprinkle on the remaining pinch of cinnamon and the reserved pecans.

No-Bake Chocolate-Hazelnut Pot de Crème

4

5 min

5 min

EQUIPMENT
1 cutting board and 1 knife
1 saucepan
4 small custard cups

INGREDIENTS

2 oz / 60 g dark chocolate
(or milk chocolate)

2 cups / 480 ml hazelnut milk
(or other nut milk)

¼ cup / 30 g cornstarch

2 tablespoons unsweetened
cocoa powder

¼ cup plus 1 tablespoon /
60 g turbinado sugar

1 pinch flaky sea salt

<u>Topping</u>
¼ cup / 20 g
hazelnuts, shelled

1 oz / 30 g
white chocolate

1 Chop the dark chocolate, hazelnuts, and white chocolate.

2 In a saucepan over medium heat, heat the hazelnut milk, cornstarch, cocoa, dark chocolate, sugar, and salt while whisking to melt the chocolate.

3 Bring to a boil while stirring continuously. Reduce the heat to low, and cook for 5 minutes; the mixture will thicken.

4 Divide evenly among custard cups. Cover with plastic wrap and refrigerate for at least 30 minutes. Serve sprinkled with hazelnuts and white chocolate pieces.

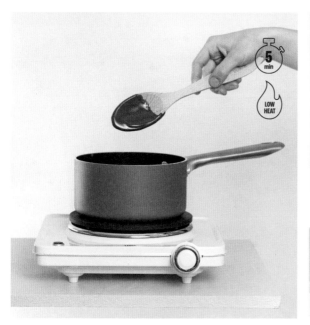

Chocolate Mousse

INGREDIENTS

Just over ¾ cup / 200 ml canned chickpea liquid (aquafaba)

¼ cup plus 2 tablespoons / 80 g sugar

7 oz / 200 g dark chocolate

1 pinch flaky sea salt

Chocolate shavings

6

15 min

EQUIPMENT

1 electric mixer
1 saucepan
4 small serving glasses
1 spatula

1 Using an electric mixer, beat the chickpea liquid for about 3 minutes while gradually adding the sugar. The mixture should become a dense foam.

2 In a double boiler or microwave set at 50% power, melt the chocolate, ensuring it does not get too hot.

3 Stirring gently, incorporate the melted chocolate and salt into the beaten chickpea liquid.

4 Spoon into glasses and refrigerate for 2 hours. Top with the chocolate shavings before serving.

Banana Pancakes

👤 **4**

🥄 **15 min**

🕐 **15 min**

EQUIPMENT
1 blender
1 stovetop

INGREDIENTS

4 ripe bananas

2 cups plus 2 tablespoons / 265 g flour

4 large / 200 g eggs

3 tablespoons / 40 g sugar (optional)

1⅛ teaspoons baking powder

1½ tablespoons unsalted butter

For the topping

2 bananas, sliced

Just over ¾ cup / 200 ml maple syrup

⅓ cup / 30 g pecans, roughly chopped

1 In a blender, blend the bananas, flour, eggs, sugar, if using, and baking powder to a smooth batter.

2 In a skillet, melt the butter. Add 1 small ladle of batter to form 4-inch / 10 cm pancakes.

3

Over high heat, cook for 1 minute on each side, or until browned. Serve with banana slices, maple syrup, and pecan pieces over the top.

Oatmeal with Plums

 4

10 min

15 min

EQUIPMENT
1 cutting board and 1 knife
1 baking dish
1 saucepan

INGREDIENTS

1 lb 5 oz / 600 g plums
4 gingersnap cookies
¼ cup / 30 g shelled pistachios
¼ cup plus 1 tablespoon / 65 g sugar
6 cups / 1.4 L whole milk
2 pinches cinnamon
4¼ cups / 400 g rolled oats
1 tablespoon crème fraîche

1 Halve the plums, remove their pits, and quarter the flesh. Chop the cookies and pistachios into large pieces.

2 Place the plums in a baking dish. Sprinkle with 3 tablespoons / 40 g of the sugar. Bake at 400°F / 200°C for 15 minutes, stirring halfway through the baking time.

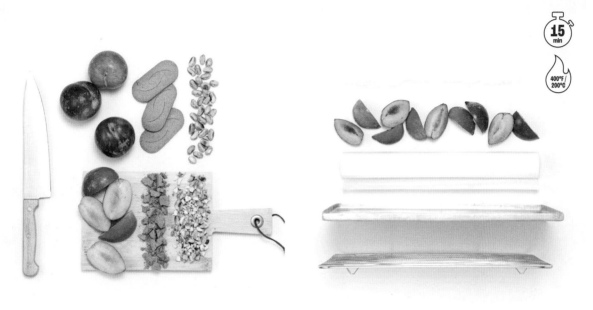

3 In a saucepan, bring the milk and 1 pinch cinnamon to a boil. Add the oats, and cook for 10 to 15 minutes at a low boil, stirring frequently. Stir in the crème fraîche and the remaining sugar at the end of the cooking time.

4 Serve the oatmeal topped with the plums and cookie and pistachio pieces.

Rustic Strawberry Tart

6

10 min

40 min

EQUIPMENT
1 cutting board and 1 knife
1 baking sheet

INGREDIENTS

1 Flaky Pastry (page 16), or use store-bought, rolled out to a large circle

For the filling
1 vanilla bean
1 lb 2 oz / 500 g strawberries
¼ cup / 30 g cornstarch
½ cup / 100 g sugar
2 tablespoons milk
2 tablespoons turbinado sugar

1 Cut the vanilla bean lengthwise in half and scrape out the seeds. Remove the strawberry stems and halve the strawberries.

2 Mix the strawberries with the cornstarch, sugar, and vanilla seeds.

3 Place the dough on a parchment paper-lined baking sheet. Fill the center with the strawberry mixture. Fold over the edges of the dough.

4 Brush the edges of the dough with the milk and sprinkle with the turbinado sugar. Bake at 400°F / 200°C for 40 minutes, or until the edges are browned and crisped. Serve warm.

Recipe Index

Index

Milk
Corn Chowder • 51
Oatmeal with Plums • 148

Mozzarella
Eggplant Parmesan • 94
Loaded Sweet Potatoes with
  White Beans • 121
Vegetables & Mozzarella • 38

Mushrooms
Winter Squash Lasagna • 126
Grilled Cheese • 44
Mushroom Bourguignon • 106
Mushroom Polenta • 58
Veggie Bolognese Pasta • 122
Veggie Burger • 68
Veggie Ramen • 84

Noodles
Veggie Ramen • 84

Oats
Oatmeal with Plums • 148

Parmesan Cheese
Celery Root Milanese • 108
Eggplant Parmesan • 94
Eggplant Rollatini • 30
Mushroom Polenta • 58
Risotto Verde • 102
Veggie Bolognese Pasta • 122

Pasta
3-Bean Minestrone • 48
Winter Squash Lasagna • 126
Pasta Salad with Candied
  Roasted Tomatoes • 56
Pasta with Leeks • 100
Veggie Bolognese Pasta • 122

Peas
Green Salad & New Potatoes • 42
Green Veggie Casserole • 130
Samosas with Peas • 26
Spring Tabbouleh • 96

Pecans
Carrot Cake • 140

Pecorino Cheese
Green Veggie Casserole • 130
Leek Pasta • 100
Lentil Shepherd's Pie • 114
Ricotta-Basil Dumplings • 74

Pesto
Pesto, Asparagus & Burrata Pizza • 62

Pizza Dough
Pesto, Asparagus & Burrata Pizza • 62

Plum
Oatmeal with Plums • 148

Potatoes
Classic Curry • 86
Corn Chowder • 51
Green Salad & New Potatoes • 42
Indian-Style Korma Curry • 89
Rösti-Style Frittata • 24
Samosas with Peas • 26
Smashed Potatoes • 36
Sweet Potato Gnocchi • 90

Vegetarian Couscous • 112
Veggie Cakes • 34

Pumpkin
Winter Squash Lasagna • 126
Squash, Spinach & Comté
  Cheese Quiche • 63

Quinoa
Red Lentils, Sweet Potato &
  Quinoa Dumplings • 74

Raclette Cheese
Smashed Potatoes • 36

Radish
Spring Tabbouleh • 96

Red Cabbage
Veggie Burger • 68

Red Lentils
Carrot & Lentil Dal • 98
Red Lentils, Sweet Potato &
  Quinoa Dumplings • 74

Red Wine
Mushroom Bourguignon • 106

Rice
Risotto Verde • 102
Vegetable Stir-Fried Rice • 92

Rice Paper Wrappers
Spring Rolls • 32

Rice Vermicelli Noodles
Spring Rolls • 32

Ricotta
Ricotta-Basil Dumplings • 74
Eggplant Rollatini • 30

Rustic Bread
Loaded Bruschetta • 20

Sandwich Bread
Grilled Cheese • 44

Savoy Cabbage
Vegetable Stir-Fried Rice • 92

Snow Peas
Green Veggie Casserole with
  Crumble Topping • 130

Spinach
3-Bean Minestrone • 48
Carrot & Lentil Dal • 98
Eggplant Rollatini • 30
Avocado-Spinach Soup • 50
Green Salad & New Potatoes • 42
Green Shakshuka • 80
Green Waffles with Eggs • 132
Squash, Spinach & Comté
  Cheese Quiche • 63
Risotto Verde • 102
Veggie Ramen • 84

Strawberries
Rustic Strawberry Tart • 150

String Beans
3-Bean Minestrone • 48

Sweet Potatoes
Golden Soup • 51
Lentil Shepherd's Pie • 114
Loaded Sweet Potatoes with
  White Beans • 121
Red Lentils, Sweet Potato &
  Quinoa Dumplings • 74
Sweet Potato Gnocchi • 90
Thai Curry 88

Tahini
Baba Ghanoush • 22

Tofu
Mushroom Bourguignon • 106
Spring Rolls • 32

Tomato Purée
Eggplant Parmesan • 94
Lentil Shepherd's Pie • 114

Tomato Sauce
Ricotta-Basil Dumplings • 74

Tomatoes
3-Bean Minestrone • 48
Carrot & Lentil Dal • 98
Chili Sin Carne • 78
Greek Salad • 54
Guacamole • 23
Loaded Bruschetta • 20
Pasta Salad with Candied
  Roasted Tomatoes • 56
Roasted Peppers & Tomatoes Soup • 50
Tex-Mex Stuffed Bell Peppers • 118
Tomato Tatin • 60
Vegetable Tian • 76
Veggie Bolognese Pasta • 122

Turnips
Vegetarian Couscous • 112

Watermelon
Greek Salad • 54

White Beans
3-Bean Minestrone • 48
Loaded Sweet Potatoes with
  White Beans • 121

Winter Squash
Winter Squash Lasagna • 126
Golden Soup • 51
Hasselback Butternut Squash• 52

Zucchini
Carrot & Lentil Dal • 98
Classic Curry • 86
Goat Cheese & Zucchini
  Casserole • 124
Green Shakshuka • 80
Halloumi Wraps 40
Indian-Style Korma Curry • 89
Vegetable Tian • 76
Vegetables & Mozzarella • 38
Vegetarian Couscous • 112
Veggie Cakes • 34

Hardie Grant

NORTH AMERICA

Hardie Grant North America
2912 Telegraph Ave
Berkeley, CA 94705

hardiegrant.com

Published in the United States by Hardie Grant North America, an imprint of
Hardie Grant Publishing Pty Ltd.

Library of Congress Cataloging-in-Publication Data is available upon request.
ISBN: 9781964786087
ISBN: 9781964786094 (eBook)

Printed in CHINA
Design by Jérôme Cousin and Nicolas Galy for NoOok
Translation by Zachary R. Townsend
Typesetting by Monica Lo
First Edition